The End of Guilt

Realizing Your Innocence through
A Course in Miracles

by Edwin Navarro

The End of Guilt

Realizing Your Innocence
through
A Course in Miracles

by Edwin Navarro

Published by Navarro Publishing

Cover design by thecovercounts.com

theendofguilt.com

Also by Edwin Navarro,

*It's All Mind: The Simplified Philosophy of
A Course in Miracles*

*Roland's Quest: A Modern-Day
Spiritual Journey*

To Ken
my teacher, my inspiration, my friend

Contents

Introduction   1

Chapter 1 What Is Guilt?   5

Chapter 2 A Brief History of Guilt   15

Chapter 3 The Rules-Based Life   32

Chapter 4 The Philosophy of *A Course in Miracles*   43

Chapter 5 Guilt and *A Course in Miracles*   57

Chapter 6 Releasing Our Guilt through Forgiveness   68

Chapter 7 The Guiltless Life   85

Chapter 8 The End of Guilt   93

Suggested Reading   95

Note: This book contains quotes from *A Course in Miracles*, which are referenced using the following shorthand,

First Letter – T for Text, W for Workbook, M for Manual for Teachers

For Text quotes, the T is followed by the Chapter, Section, and Paragraph numbers.

For Workbook quotes, the W is followed by the Lesson and Paragraph numbers.

For Manual quotes, the M is followed by the Chapter and Paragraph numbers.

Examples: T-11.VI.7, W-169.5, M-21.1

Introduction

Depending on who you listen to, guilt is either a necessary limiter to one's behavior, or a severe debilitating psychological problem. In the first case, we worry that if we don't feel any sense of guilt, we would be out of control, with no moral sense. In fact, we often use terms like sociopath for someone who feels no guilt.

On the other hand, we consider extremes of guilt to be a psychological problem, often rendering an individual unable to function normally in society. Such a person will see judgment at every turn, and may never believe there is a way to lead a normal life.

We talk about the weight of guilt, how it pulls us down, how we're tied to those events in our past for which we judge ourselves harshly. Memories of painful experiences, and most importantly, our part in the creation of that pain are present in everyone who lives in this world.

'If only' and 'I should have' are the mantras of the guilty person as one's life is re-examined continuously. It seems as if only time can heal the guilt in our lives, but often time simply covers it over with other events, and what was thought to be long past can resurface.

But where does this guilt come from? In this book, we will look at guilt from many different angles, dissecting it into its component parts, and ultimately realizing how it is created. Once we recognize these mechanisms, we will discover a powerful answer to guilt.

The Rules of Life

In most systems of thought, there exists a set of rules we are meant to live by. Whether these rules grow out of religion or philosophy, or are simply passed down through the generations, they represent the core beliefs with which we make decisions every day.

We live with a set of rules in our minds which guide our behavior. Everyone's rules are a little different, so in some cases we might judge someone else's behavior differently than we would judge ourselves. For instance, we might excuse a behavior in a child that we wouldn't excuse in ourselves.

Though everyone carries these rules around with them, if asked to explain why we did something, sometimes we don't actually know and will even make up reasons that seem to make sense. We often feel guilty about actions we have taken without understanding why what we did feels wrong.

Ultimately, though, we will at some point along the way violate one or more of the rules in our minds, and the result will be feelings of guilt. These guilty feelings seem to have a real stickiness to them, often living in our minds throughout our whole lives.

It appears the only way to eliminate guilt is not to violate the rules that would cause us to feel guilty. Oddly though, no one ever seems to be able to completely avoid violating these rules. Even people we consider the saints, the gurus, the high priests, all seem to have failings, leaving us mere mortals to despair of ever leading a guilt-free life.

A Course in Miracles

This book is based on a powerful system of thought called *A Course in Miracles*. The Course, as we will refer to it, was written during the years 1965 to 1972 and was first published in 1976. It consists of three parts – a text, a workbook for students, and a manual for teachers, all totaling over 1000 pages. The text and the manual are to be read and studied, while the workbook consists of 365 daily lessons that provide a more direct experience and application of the ideas from the text.

The Course was written by Helen Schucman, a clinical psychologist who worked at several hospitals in New York. In describing how the Course was created, she refers to herself as a scribe, writing what came to her at different times of the day, always in a fully conscious state. She was able to stop the scribing process whenever she wanted and immediately return to it when she was ready. The author of the Course says he is Jesus, and it is written from the perspective of a teacher.

For the purposes of this book, the process of the creation of the Course is not important. What is important is the system of thought, the philosophy presented in the Course. We will use that philosophy and apply it to our subject of guilt, and see how the principles and concepts contained in that philosophy will first show us where our guilt truly comes from, and then how we can free ourselves.

The End of Guilt

We will begin our discussions by defining guilt as precisely as we can, looking deep into its eyes, and finding those mechanisms that create our guilt. We will look at examples, from simple personal guilt to the weight of societal and moral guilt.

Next we will explore guilt from a historical perspective, looking at the ancient and modern religions which provide the moral rules for many people in our societies. We will look at how the great philosophers incorporated guilt and morality into their systems of thought. Finally we will examine guilt from the point of view of modern psychology.

With this background, we will see how the rules in our minds guide our everyday decisions, and how by constantly violating those rules in ways, both great and small, we build our edifice of internal guilt.

Once we understand guilt in all its aspects, we will introduce the philosophy of the Course. With this as our basis we will re-examine guilt in a new light, discovering its illusory nature. Through the practice of forgiveness, we will see how we can free ourselves of each instance of guilt, one at a time.

Finally we will examine what it means to live a life without guilt. How will the world look through the eyes of a guiltless person? How would such a person operate in the world? What would be the moral code that would guide them? What if everyone lived this way?

So let's begin the journey from the pain of our lives to the end of guilt.

Chapter 1

What Is Guilt?

Before we can look at ways to eliminate guilt from our lives, we first need to define exactly what guilt is. For most people guilty feelings are easily recognizable, though if asked to define guilt, they may be more likely to describe guilt in reference to a particular act than in the abstract.

We will be looking for a broad, general definition of guilt that will encompass the guilty feelings that most people experience, including other experiences similar to guilt, such as shame and regret. We are limited, though, by the use of words, which the Course refers to as "symbols of symbols... thus twice removed from reality" (M-21.1). We will use words to try to describe our experience, knowing the experience will always be beyond the words.

In common usage, the word guilt actually has two different meanings. It can refer to a judgment imposed on someone by an outside agent, be it a legal system or religious organization, or from another individual. Throughout history, all societies have had some concept of crime and punishment. In some cases the guilt or innocence of an individual is determined by religious authorities, sometimes by appointed or elected judges, and sometimes by lay members of society.

In all these cases the judgment is externally applied, and if the judged individual is part of that society, he is expected to abide by these decisions. Even if the person being judged does not consciously feel guilty, he must deal with the externally decreed judgment of his guilt, and accept the imposed punishment.

5

If the judgment comes instead from an individual, we can have different reactions to this judgment – we could accept the judgment and feel guilty; we could reject the judgment and try to convince the other person they are wrong to judge us; or we might simply ignore the judgment, feeling it was misguided in some way. If we accept the judgment, then we are accepting the guilt that comes with it.

The other meaning of guilt, and the one most important to this book, is the internal feeling of guilt for offenses we believe we have committed. In this case there need not be an external judgment – we are judging ourselves based on our beliefs about the ethical and moral rules that govern our lives. The offense we believe we have committed may or may not rise to the level of a societal crime.

Often in interpersonal relationships, we feel we may have treated someone poorly in an emotional way. These acts can lead to very deep-seated feelings of guilt, but may never be judged by any external agency or person. In this book, since we will ultimately be focused on the mind and changes in one's life through changes in mind, we will be primarily concerned with the internal sense of guilt.

Later we will actually see that due to the core principle of projection as presented in the Course, there really is no difference between the externally imposed judgments and the internally felt guilt. For now though, we will focus on the second meaning, on our internal feelings of guilt, and how we can define the word guilt in a useful way. We will then explore common examples of guilt in our everyday lives, and look at how some other concepts, like shame, fit into our definition.

A Definition of Guilt

For our purposes, we want to use a broad definition of guilt, one which will include as many of the unpleasant inner feelings we experience. With this broad definition it is hoped that one can see how so many of our everyday actions are driven by our internal guilt, or in many cases, just the anticipation of guilt.

So we will use the following definition:

> *Guilt is feeling bad because of something*
> *we believe we did wrong.*

In order for this to be a complete definition we have to know what is meant by 'feeling bad' and 'wrong'. Here feeling bad will include any feeling of discomfort including emotional unease, a minor headache, extreme pain, severe depression, rage, worry, etc. Essentially it is any feeling that is not loving toward oneself or another, which includes a very broad range.

This idea of non-loving thoughts is one we will revisit later as part of our discussion about the Course. This is a core principle of the Course – if you are not having loving thoughts toward someone or toward yourself, you are experiencing an illusory thought, one you will be able to free yourself of through the practice of forgiveness.

For now, simply assume that any emotional experience you have which is not centered on love is one that will be included in our sense of 'feeling bad'. Think about how you are feeling toward someone and if there is something other than love, caring, compassion toward that person, then you are having a 'bad' feeling as referenced in our definition. We will expand this concept further once we have explored the philosophy of the Course.

That covers the first part of our definition, so now let's look at the second part. Defining 'wrong' is a bit more difficult, because our definition of guilt includes the word 'believe'. Therefore what is wrong is what a person believes to be wrong, which can differ greatly from person to person. This means that each individual will have a different set of beliefs on which to decide if an action is wrong or not.

For example, most people would say they believe that killing is wrong, but if pressed further you would find that it makes a difference what kind of killing you're talking about. Though most everyone would say cold-blooded murder is wrong, there are many who believe killing in self-defense or defense of one's loved-ones or one's country is not wrong. Most believe that killing insects, or other 'pests,' is ok, but some consider this to be wrong. Then is killing an ant purposefully and doing it accidentally equally wrong?

These rules and beliefs may seem to have come from outside us – perhaps from our church or our parents – but they are only active within our minds when we make them our own. Different individuals hearing the same sermon or lecture from some religious or other authority will decide in their own individual way whether to accept those rules. Once a rule is accepted, it can be used to determine whether our actions are right or wrong.

The important point here is that it is impossible to find a universal meaning of what people believe is wrong. Everyone has a different set of beliefs and rules in their minds that define for them what is wrong for them. In a later chapter we will explore in greater depth how we each build our internal rules – those rules through which we will decide the rightness or wrongness of our actions.

Examples of Guilt

So back to our definition. The feeling of guilt is an unpleasant feeling, one that is not loving, that exists because we believe we have done something wrong, where that something wrong is ultimately defined by our own internal beliefs. Now we will look at some examples of internal guilt and see how our definition fits those examples.

Example 1: After losing her job, Sarah goes over to see her sister, Joan, to ask her for some money to tide her over until she can find a new job. Joan flatly refuses, telling Sarah she has always been a loser. Hearing this criticism which she's heard many times before, something snaps in Sarah and she begins screaming at Joan, throwing things around the room, and then runs out of the house.

Later as she thinks about what she did, Sarah feels terrible, thinking that if she were only more successful, Joan wouldn't have been put in a situation where she had to refuse her. Here Sarah has a long history with her sister, a relationship in which she feels inferior to her. In this scenario, the years of being put in that inferior position lead her to lash out. At the same time she loves her sister and knows she has crossed a line in their relationship.

She feels bad both because she believes her sister may be right and because she knows her behavior was inappropriate. She has violated her internal rule of always being loving toward her family no matter what the situation, and also the rule of keeping her emotions under control.

Example 2: Michael and Amy have been married for several years, when over time their communication seems to break down. Feeling lonely, Michael begins a brief affair with a colleague at work. They meet after work some evenings and when Amy ultimately asks him why he's out so many nights, he lies to her, telling her he has a new project at work that demands extra time. He knows the affair is wrong, but he also feels a deeper sense of guilt because he is lying to someone he loves.

Though he may feel there are reasons for the affair, Michael can't really justify it to himself. His internal rules about marital behavior have clearly been violated. He feels a deeper guilt for lying to his wife, which violates not only marital rules, but also his sense of proper behavior toward someone he cares about.

Example 3: David is the only child of a mother who has cancer and is slowly dying. He's married with three teenage children, a demanding job, and struggles financially. He doesn't believe he can adequately take care of his mother and he doesn't want his wife to be burdened with her care. He decides to place his mother in a nursing home, where she is unhappy and where she ultimately dies. He knows he should have done more to make her last years good ones.

He can rationalize that having a difficult job and being a husband and father takes all of his time and energy, and there was nothing else he could do about his mother. On the other hand he also knows that his mother made many sacrifices throughout his life so he could grow up to be the man he is today.

Realizing this, David feels he really should have sacrificed something in his life to create the time to be with his mother when she needed him. Her death means he can never resolve this with his mother, and he may carry this guilt for the rest of his life.

Example 4: Melissa goes out to celebrate her twenty-first birthday with friends. She knows they have all had too much to drink, but when her friend, Susan, asks her to drive home, she doesn't feel she can refuse her. On the way home, the car goes off the road and hits a tree and Susan is killed. Melissa is later charged with manslaughter.

Here a simple and, at the time, seemingly harmless decision is made that ends up wrecking many lives. Melissa has violated the basic tenets of her religious beliefs, as well as the laws of her society. She not only must deal with her internal guilt, but also with guilt imposed by Susan's family, the community at-large, and the legal system.

Whether she goes to prison or not, she will be imprisoned by her guilt, knowing she has taken the life of someone she cared about. Though the decision seemed simple at the time, it may have lifelong debilitating consequences.

We will revisit these examples later in the book to see how we can apply the concepts of the Course. We will look at the ultimate source of the guilt in all these cases, as well as ways it can be released.

What Is Guilt?

Similar Concepts

Those who explore different cultures in the world discover there are many words used to describe the guilt and shame we all experience. In Asian cultures there is more emphasis on the concept of shame, and there are often multiple words used to describe different types of shame.

In Western culture, especially Catholic and Jewish traditions, the emphasis is on guilt and how guilt can lead one to examine one's behavior. It is hoped that through this examination a person can understand what wrong actions were taken, and thereby change the behavior that brought about the guilty feelings.

Modern psychologists have tried to show how guilt, shame, regret, embarrassment, and similar feelings are all different and should be treated differently. We will take the opposite approach, and conclude that these are all different aspects of the same feeling and the same problem. We will lump them all together under the term guilt.

Before we take this generalist approach, however, it is useful to look at these different terms and see how, at least in the English language, these aspects differ. We will then see how we can put them together under the banner of guilt and focus our attention on this general term in order to find the cause and the cure for guilt.

In all these different terms and definitions, there is one common factor – we feel bad about something we did. How we express that may vary, so that whether we describe our experience as regret, shame, embarrassment, or guilt, in all cases there is the common sense of having done something wrong, and feeling bad about it.

Embarrassment

In most cases, we are embarrassed when we violate some social convention. Unlike guilt and shame, embarrassment usually results in a strong physical response, such as a diverted gaze or blushing. There must be an audience for one to be embarrassed, whereas shame and guilt can be felt when one is alone.

The transgression that leads to embarrassment can seem trivial – forgetting someone's name when trying to introduce them; arriving at a party over- or under-dressed; trying to impress someone and saying something stupid; or stumbling and dropping some groceries. Embarrassment can also stem from our and our society's attitudes toward the body. Bodily functions, nudity, or sexual talk can all lead to embarrassing situations.

In most cases the embarrassment is transitory – eventually we stop blushing and often we can later laugh about the situation. When embarrassment leads to self-criticism – 'I was such an idiot' – feelings of guilt and shame can grow. In this case the original embarrassment was transitory, but the individual's fixation on the event can lead to long-term feelings of guilt or shame.

Regret

We feel regret when we think of something we have lost or failed to attain. Regret is feeling bad over something we didn't do rather than something we did. 'I wish I'd gone to college.' 'I wish I'd said something to her.' These are the 'what-ifs' of life – 'what if I'd only done it differently.'

Where regret is differentiated from guilt is in whether the person feels they were responsible for what happened. Was the reason for not going to college because there was no opportunity, or did the person choose not to go? What we will see later in our discussions of the Course is that these are really equivalent, and ultimately we are all responsible for what appears to only happen to us.

Shame

Like guilt, which has an externally imposed meaning and an internal meaning, the word shame is used in several different ways in the English language. In one usage, it is synonymous with guilt – 'I feel ashamed about what I said to her' and 'I feel guilty about what I said to her.' These two statements are essentially the same.

In Eastern cultures, especially certain Asian cultures, the concept of shame is very important to the functioning of the family and of the community. When one commits an act against the wishes of family or community, that person is expected to feel shame and to exhibit the proper behavior for one who is ashamed. We'll explore this further in the next chapter when we look at how different cultures treat the concepts of guilt and shame.

In another case of shame, young people often feel ashamed of their bodies. In these cases, it's not easy to substitute guilt for shame, because there is no clear act that led to these feelings, as there is in the case of guilt. So shame is used where the bad feelings seem to come from an internal state, rather than an external act.

In modern psychology, an effort is made to distinguish guilt, which is perceived as healthy if not overdone, and shame, which is considered unhealthy. Here the differentiation is that guilt is the result of a wrong act, whereas shame is the result of a lack of self-worth or self-esteem. It's expected that the person feeling guilty can work through their feelings much more easily than someone experiencing shame. Again we'll explore this more in the next chapter.

From these discussions, it appears that the concepts of shame, regret, and embarrassment have nuances that differentiate them from guilt, and in common usage this is true. But we said at the beginning of this section that all these concepts can be included in our definition of guilt.

In all these cases we are experiencing unpleasant feelings, 'feeling bad,' but it appears that not all of the concepts require that we believe we have done something wrong. The key to bringing all of these concepts together will be the chapter on the philosophy of the Course. In that chapter we will discover the source of these feelings, and how that source is the same no matter what non-loving feelings we are experiencing. Finally we will learn how forgiveness can be applied to free us from all of these emotions.

Chapter 2

A Brief History of Guilt

Now that we have established our definition of guilt, in the next two chapters we will examine how we acquire the beliefs and rules that help us determine what is right and wrong. This determination is key to how we make decisions, and ultimately to whether or not we feel guilty about those decisions.

In this chapter we will examine belief systems from a historical perspective, looking at the religious and philosophical traditions that have influenced societies and individuals. We will focus specifically on how those traditions view the concept of guilt, shedding light on the process through which we internalize those beliefs.

In the next chapter, these concepts will be expanded to look at all the influences that affect the way we acquire the rules to live by – from our parents, our peers, media, politics, and ultimately our own individual experience living in this world.

The exploration in this chapter will necessarily be a broad overview of these religious and philosophical traditions rather than an in-depth study. The purpose is to look at how different societies have addressed the question of guilt, and to look at some of the influences from these traditions we might find in our own lives that can lead to feelings of guilt.

Though we will find that different systems of thought put a varying amount of emphasis on guilt, it is important to understand we are operating throughout this book on the assumption that guilt is a universal individual experience. Everyone living in this world will feel guilt at some time during this life, whether that guilt is consciously recognized or not.

We will begin with the three Western religions – Judaism, Christianity, and Islam, followed by the Eastern religions – Hinduism, Buddhism, and Confucianism. Then we will examine the Western philosophical traditions and finally modern psychology.

Judaism

Judaic tradition is centered in the Law. A devout Jew tries to observe the Law, and when one fails, a sin is committed. As in our discussion above, guilt here has two meanings – the person is judged guilty by the Jewish religious society (and ultimately by God) for having broken the Law, and the person will feel internal guilt for this transgression.

The Law that is followed comes from the Hebrew scriptures and is considered to be a given to a devout Jew. There is no need for faith or any kind of external proof, only for observance of the Law. Ultimately it is assumed this Law comes from God, and violations of the Law are acts against God. The religious authorities in Judaism tend to be more concerned with legal interpretations of this Law than with priestly duties.

Once a violation has occurred and one's guilt has been established, either externally or internally, the person is expected to atone for the sin. Historically this has involved sacrifice of some sort, though today that sacrifice may not take a physical form, but will more likely be an internal repentance and an attempt to make right the wrong that occurred. This involves asking for forgiveness from God as well.

There is an assumption in Judaism that each of us has an internal sense of moral right and wrong, but that it is not always clear – therefore the need for Jewish Laws to help guide us in our actions. Once these Laws have been learned, one will know when a violation has occurred and will take appropriate actions to atone for the guilt. As in most secular laws, it is not an excuse that you did not understand the Law. Through education in the Hebrew scriptures, every Jew should know the right way to act.

In today's world, as with all religions, we see a great spectrum of beliefs – from the Orthodox Jews at one end to the secular Jews at the other. Orthodox Jews practice more of the cultish rituals, especially focusing on dietary laws and observance of special times and days. The secular Jews may have only limited observance of any of these practices, but will often still try to follow the Jewish moral code.

The concept of Jewish guilt has also become part of our popular culture in the writings of Jewish authors and movies like those of Woody Allen. The Jewish mother has become almost a caricature for externally-induced guilt in our society. Though these popular depictions may take it to the extreme, guilt is a core principle in Judaism and how one's own guilt and the guilt of others is handled will ultimately determine one's relationship with God.

Christianity

Christian ideas about guilt and sin have changed over the centuries. This evolution began with the Biblical Jesus, was made into a formal structure through the writings of Paul and Augustine, and then was transformed by Martin Luther, which led to the great split between Western Catholicism and Protestantism.

The Christian church today is made up of over 500 sects spread around the world, so it is reasonable to assume that attitudes toward guilt will vary significantly among Christians. Historically it is useful, though, to follow the development of these ideas in the Roman Catholic church and then see how these ideas were changed through the Reformation.

In the accounts of Jesus' life in the Bible, he does not use the word guilt, but does speak often of sin. It would be reasonable to assume that when he talks about sin, some type of guilt is implied, whether external or internal. He takes the concept of sin to a higher level than in the Old Testament, referring to thoughts about sinful actions as sinful themselves.

On the other hand he does elevate the concept of forgiveness in such a way that everyone is provided with a path to absolve themselves of their guilt. There is an implication in Jesus' teachings that one can, through seeking forgiveness from another and seeking forgiveness from God, wipe the slate of sin and guilt clean.

It was then up to Paul in the later writings of the New Testament to provide more structure to these teachings. Specifically Paul came up with the idea of Original Sin – Adam's sin in eating the forbidden fruit is inherited by everyone, which means everyone is guilty before they ever commit a sin in this life. Paul saw Christ as the second Adam, and through him and his teachings, this Original Sin could be reversed, freeing us of our guilt. Paul suffered guilt himself and wrote extensively about sexual matters and marriage, carrying Jesus' teachings into new, more specific arenas.

In the centuries since Paul, many writers have expanded on these doctrines, one of the most influential being Augustine, born in the 4th century. Augustine took the doctrines of the time and expanded them to the point where guilt became a central aspect of the church. Original Sin was a given, and through being baptized in the Roman Catholic church, one could erase this sin. But this did not eliminate sin, for Augustine believed there were dark forces within each of us, including sexual urges, that were essentially beyond our control.

The remedy to all of this was the penitential system. First, one must recognize one's sins and regret them – in other words, one must experience one's guilt fully. Next was confession to a priest, and finally there must be some sort of restitution, which can take the form of specific prayers of forgiveness or in more practical ways, actual repaying of debts, either physically or emotionally.

These were the doctrines of the Western Christian church up to the 16th century, and form the core of the modern Roman Catholic church. In the early 1500's, however, Martin Luther, in an attempt to reform the existing church, proposed a radical new philosophy. Luther made the Bible the sole authority, bypassing the edicts of the Catholic priesthood. Everyone could approach God directly – there was no longer the need for priestly confession. Instead one could pray directly to God and receive His forgiveness.

These radical writings led to the Protestant Reformation which leads to the Christian church we have today – Roman and Orthodox Catholicism and a myriad of Protestant sects, each with a unique interpretation of the Biblical teachings. Yet in spite of all the variability in teachings, the concepts of sin, guilt, and forgiveness are central throughout the Christian church.

Islam

The religion of Islam began in the 7th century through the teachings of the prophet Muhammad. The holy book, called the Qur'an, is believed by Muslims to be the literal word of God and was revealed to Muhammad. They believe there were previous prophets, including Moses, Abraham, and Jesus, but the teachings from these prophets had become distorted, and the Qur'an is God's final revelation. The Qur'an in Arabic is considered the true word of God, and all other translations are only interpretations.

In Islam, God is the ultimate end. Pre-Islamic society was not one of evil, but one of ignorance and ingratitude. Islam means submission to God, a submission that is total and irrevocable for a devout Muslim. There are five pillars, or essential acts, in the Islamic faith. These are the creed ("I testify there are no deities other than God alone and I testify that Muhammad is the Messenger of God."), the five daily ritual prayers, fasting from dawn to dusk during Ramadan, alms-giving or helping the poor and needy, and a pilgrimage to Mecca at least once in one's lifetime.

Sin in Islam is willfully acting in opposition to God's will, and is considered to be more a weakness than something evil. What actions are sinful are spelled out in the Qur'an, and there is always the possibility of asking for God's forgiveness for one's sins. Each person can go to God alone, since there is no need for any priestly intervention. There is no concept of Original Sin in Islam – Adam and Eve were simply misguided.

In a way similar to that of Judaism, Islamic law governs how one should behave, and violations of that law lead to guilt, more focused on external guilt or culpability, rather than feelings of internal guilt. The Qur'an is a guide for individuals to help them morally choose right from wrong. When a person becomes aware of his own guilt, the emphasis is not to dwell on guilt, but to release it through repentance and returning to God.

Muslims believe in free will, and like in Judaism and Christianity, this means constantly making moral choices in our lives, choices that affect our relationship to God. It is understood that we will on occasion disobey God, but we can ask for mercy and forgiveness. The one thing God will not forgive is ingratitude for all the mercies God has given us.

In the Qur'an, divine forgiveness is key. It is an essential attribute of God and of the Prophet, and is to be emulated by all followers of the faith. It begins with a recognition of the transgression, whether this is realized by the individual or shown by an external authority. Then one must have a change of heart and ask for God's forgiveness, as well as providing compensation to anyone harmed by the act. Practically Muslims are not unlike others in feeling guilty about acts they have committed and seeking resolution and redemption for this guilt.

Hinduism

Hinduism is one of the oldest religions in the world, and through the ages, it has evolved into different sects and traditions. Modern Hindus observe many different forms of Hinduism; from devotion to multiple deities, to yogic practices, to focus on good works, to meditation, and a variety of other forms.

There are many ancient writings, the Vedas, which represent the foundation of Hindu belief. After the Vedas, came a whole host of other writings, including the Upanishads, and perhaps the most important work in modern Hinduism, the Bhagavad-Gita.

A Brief History of Guilt

This was written after the time of Buddha and around the time of Christ, and consists of a series of dialogs between the warrior Arjuna and the god Krishna. These dialogs represent a concise presentation of the Hindu philosophy.

Two important concepts in Hinduism are karma and dharma. Hindus believe in reincarnation, the cycle of death and rebirth. Karma represents a natural process of cause and effect, wherein one can, through right actions, eventually be free of this cycle. Conversely through wrong moral actions one may descend the ladder of rebirth to a lower standing in the next life.

Dharma is conformity to a moral duty that is inherent in all living things. It includes the rituals one must undertake in life, as well as one's vocation and one's relationships with others. It represents all that is right and good in the universe, and living in accordance with dharma brings one closer to personal liberation.

The moral traditions of Western religions are focused on the impact an individual's actions have on another. In Hinduism and Buddhism, a person follows a moral path in order to better oneself. This means that the concepts of guilt and shame are viewed differently in Hinduism. Hindus may feel guilt over actions they have taken, but the resolution of that guilt is not a focus of the religion. What is important is that one recognize what one did, and try to act better in the future. There is no Western concept of a formal repentance.

Because of the strong emphasis on family and community in the Hindu culture, there can be a sense of shame when one acts against the wishes of this community. The way to deal with this shame is to understand what wrong was done and the impact it had on others in the family or community, and then to vow to act differently.

As we stated before, guilt is a universal experience, whether you are conscious of it or not. Even though the Hindu religion does not emphasize guilt in the way it is in Western religions, this does not mean that Hindus do not experience guilt. There are still moral rules one must follow and individuals will feel guilty when these are violated. What differs is the means that are prescribed in Hinduism to resolve your guilt.

Buddhism

Siddhartha Gautama (later known as the Buddha) lived sometime between the 6th and 5th centuries BC. He grew up in a life of privilege, but after attaining adulthood, he observed suffering in the world and decided to dedicate his life to understanding this suffering and finding a path to liberation. He went on a spiritual quest trying a variety of different practices and concluded the right path was the Middle Way, which came somewhere between everyday life and the life of the extreme ascetic.

This path included regular meditation and compassion for all life. He famously achieved enlightenment while meditating under a sacred fig tree, the Bodhi tree. He eventually started a monastic order and it was through his oral teachings that we learn of his philosophy. The first writings of Buddhism did not appear until two centuries after the Buddha died, and therefore there are no divinely inspired writings in Buddhism.

In Buddhism there is no God as Westerners think of God. Instead there is the state of Nirvana, a state of emptiness where all dualities disappear. It is a state that is impossible to describe in words and must be experienced through meditation. Consequently there is no God to please or displease and no God to judge a person's behavior.

Buddha teaches the four Noble Truths – the existence of suffering, how suffering is caused by attachment, how suffering ends when we liberate attachments, and the path to achieving that liberation. The path is referred to as the Eightfold Path – right views, right intent, right speech, right conduct, right livelihood, right effort, mindfulness, and concentration.

Karma exists in Buddhism in a way similar to Hinduism. Through following the path to liberation, one can end the cycle of death and rebirth. This is achieved both through inner meditation and right action in the world.

Since there is no judgmental God in Buddhism, there is no sense of absolute guilt for violating some law of God. Instead one observes one's own actions as to whether those actions increase or decrease suffering. That suffering may be in the external world or within oneself. Guilt is just another attachment – in this case, an attachment to a past event and the negative emotions associated with that event.

A person can end his guilt through meditation and especially by focusing on the present. Every action and every change that is possible must happen in the present. Dwelling on past events or worrying about future events is merely a smokescreen that prevents us from seeing the present clearly. Once one learns to live in the present, guilt becomes a meaningless emotion.

So practitioners of Buddhism may on occasion have feelings of guilt, shame, or regret, but these should just be viewed as emotional attachments like so many others. One should simply follow the practice to release these guilty feelings.

Confucianism

There has been debate for centuries about how to classify Confucianism. Since there is no deity and no description of a world beyond this one, it is difficult to call it a religion. It is an ethical philosophy, but one that has permeated the Chinese society in such a way that it is hard to distinguish between the teachings of Confucius and ordinary societal norms. As a philosophy, it is closest to the Western ideas of humanism.

Confucius was born in 551 BC and lived into his 70's. As an adult he originally pursued a government career, but was only mildly successful. Eventually he started a school to train young men for public service, and it was out of these teachings that his philosophy developed. He left only very brief writings, but one hundred years later, one of his disciples, Mencius, wrote a book of sayings, called the Book of Mencius, which has become the core text of Confucianism.

The concept of virtue is central to Confucianism. One should lead a life of positive moral duty, a life of warm-hearted expression, charity, and compassion toward one's fellow man. This sense of duty starts toward one's family, and extends to the wider community, including not only the immediate community where one lived, but also the wider community of the world. One is expected to be honest in all of one's dealings with others, and always speaking the truth. Confucianism even includes a Golden Rule – Do not do to others what you do not want them to do to you.

Along with this sense of moral duty, a person must have the capacity for guilt and shame, or else there would be no sense of remorse when one has failed in a particular duty. So unlike the other Eastern schools of thought, guilt and especially shame play an important role in Confucianism. There are several kinds of guilt – failure to fulfill a positive duty (similar to regret), doing something morally wrong (internal guilt), and breaking the law (external guilt). There are also different types of shame, those differences being much more subtle than in the Western concept of shame.

Since Confucianism has no God from whom one can ask for forgiveness, everyone is personally responsible for their own actions, and in order to relieve themselves of guilt and shame, steps must be taken to right whatever wrongs have occurred. Since shame is so central to the philosophy, one does not talk about problems in public – they are to be dealt with in private among family and friends.

When a person feels that he has offended someone, it is expected he will accept responsibility and learn from the experience. One can express regret to another verbally or through a proper silence, something the offended person will know is a sign of regret. Then the offender must resolve to act in a more moral, appropriate way in the future.

So in Confucianism, the meaning of life comes from practical, everyday living, and not through a promised experience of God or a greater life beyond this one. This makes it unique among the six traditions we have explored so far.

The Philosophy of Reason

We will now examine guilt in the context of the philosophy of reason, the tradition that began in ancient Greece and gained momentum with the Renaissance and a new scientific, materialist view of the world. In a way similar to Confucianism, these philosophies seek to find a path to leading a moral, happy life without the absoluteness of God and religion.

It was the teachings of Socrates that began this focus on reason in Greek philosophy, and it was Plato who first put the teachings into writing. Plato was Socrates' pupil and he wrote down the dialogs Socrates would have with his students. Plato carried the philosophy beyond these basic tenets and started a school in which Aristotle was a student. Aristotle then made this philosophy so complete in his writings that it remained influential for almost two thousand years.

The basis of the philosophy is virtue and the ultimate good is happiness, not just the simple bodily pleasure, but a full intellectual and emotional happiness derived from the pursuit of excellence. The rewards were for this life, not for a relationship with God or for an afterlife. Through this pursuit, one seeks to live a life of honor, courage, and nobility of character. One avoids extremes and tries to find a middle path, using our basic goodness and conscience as a guide.

Guilt, as in Confucianism, is the result of our failure to follow our conscience, to act out of pure self-interest, or to harm another in our pursuit of happiness. Aristotle recognized that there were no absolutes in this philosophy, so there is no simple set of moral laws one can refer to. Everything becomes situational to an extent, which makes the decisions more difficult than when there is a religious authority to guide us. When one's decisions lead to less happiness for oneself or others, guilt and shame will occur, and these will help guide us in future decisions.

Following the fall of Greek culture and later the Roman Empire, the Middle Ages were a time dominated by religious thought, and the philosophy of reason took a backseat in the Western world. With the dawn of the Renaissance in the 1400's, reason, and especially the ideas of science came to the forefront. For the next four hundred years, there was a flowering of philosophical thought.

Many philosophers gained great fame through this period, but we will focus on three here to give a flavor of the thinking of the time – Immanuel Kant, John Stuart Mill, and Freidrich Nietzsche. All three addressed the concept of guilt, but from very different perspectives.

Immanuel Kant lived in the 1600's and has been called the philosopher's philosopher. He spent his life seeking a universal system of thought. His most famous contribution is the 'categorical imperative,' which says 'Act as if the maxim of your action were to become through your will a universal law of nature.' This could be considered a more sophisticated version of the Golden Rule – we act in the way we want everyone to act. As with all versions of the Golden Rule, Kant found some exceptions, rules that were absolute in his mind.

Kant believed in the idea of the conscience as a judge, as something incorporated into our very being. If we act against our conscience, we will experience guilt. He wanted to focus more on our culpability for violating a moral law, than on our feelings of guilt, since his philosophy always saw reason as primary and feelings as secondary. Ultimately our acts should come from duty, not from fear of guilt, whether internal or external. He also had to accept that there might be a higher moral power, some form of God, in order for this moral imperative to have a root cause.

A Brief History of Guilt

In the 18th century, the philosophy of utilitarianism was first espoused by Jeremy Bentham, but it was John Stuart Mill in the 19th century who carried the philosophy the furthest. The basic idea is that pleasure is the ultimate good, and the act that causes the most good for the most people is the moral act. Pleasure here is not just hedonistic pleasure, but includes the pleasurable feelings of altruism and good works. It underpins the political concepts of democracy, where the correct political path should provide the most good to the most people.

Mill discusses remorse, which is the same as our definition of guilt, as the ultimate sanction that enforces moral behavior. Our feelings of remorse teach us which acts we should avoid, and the experience of pleasure teaches us which we should encourage. Unlike Kant, Mill did not resort to God or religion as a source of morality, but believed it was a basic part of human nature. Ultimately utilitarianism can lead to a simplistic do-it-yourself morality, and a selfish one as well.

This brings us to Friedrich Nietzsche, who could be called the anti-guilt philosopher. Nietzsche lived in Germany at the end of the 19th century. His writings were edited by his anti-Semitic sister, leading to a perception that he was also anti-Semitic and in favor of German militarism, which wasn't true. His philosophy is about the individual as a powerful, heroic figure, autonomous and free, with reason as his guide. His ideas were a reaction to the moralism of Judeo-Christian traditions.

The human is a heroic figure, whose purpose is happiness through productive achievement and with reason as the only absolute. Guilt is the arch enemy, a legacy of fire and brimstone Christianity. We must question all beliefs, and ultimately power and the instinct for freedom determines our happiness. Along with this power comes responsibility, which Nietzsche equates to a good conscience, in contrast to what he called the bad conscience, our sense of guilt at having violated externally-imposed moral rules.

Modern Psychology

From ancient times to the early 19th century, the study of the mind was considered to be the purview of philosophy. As we saw, philosophers address questions of thought, emotion, morality, and how we as humans make decisions, all aspects of the mind. Included in this philosophy of the mind is the role of guilt in one's personality.

The term 'psychology' was first used in the 16th century, but was not widely used until the late 18th century. Often the term 'mental philosophy' was used, but beginning in the late 19th century psychology became the accepted term, and an attempt was made to use more scientific principles in this study. This was the beginning of psychology as a discipline separate from philosophy.

Throughout Europe and America, a new field of experimental psychology evolved. Tests were devised to measure the performance and reactions of different individuals when given a particular task or stimulus. By measuring these responses across a large number of people, statistical averages of behavior could be determined, and hypotheses of the behavior of the mind could be formed and tested.

Some of these psychologists wanted to measure only the exterior behavior of these individuals and others wanted to understand the thinking processes that led to a particular response. This ultimately created a split among the experimental psychologists that persists to the modern day. Those focusing on only external behavior formed the field of behaviorism, and those considering the internal mental processes formed the field of cognitive psychology. Other branches and sub-branches of psychology have come and gone over the last century.

For most modern psychologists, guilt is inherent in all of us. Though there are those who are identified as sociopathic, without guilt, even here there is often acceptance that guilt may simply be subconscious. Guilt is the result of violating the social norms and religious tenets of the society in which one lives. Guilt becomes a necessary limiter to one's behavior, allowing the individual to take notice of wrong behavior and to hopefully correct that behavior.

If a person were truly without guilt, it is assumed that he would act in a way detrimental to the society and to himself. Therefore some level of guilt is considered to be not only acceptable, but a positive trait. Too much guilt, however, can lead one to depression and anxiety and an overall negative self-image. If one acts without guilt, the psychological therapist will try to show the individual the consequences of his actions and thereby instill some level of guilt. If one is too guilty, the therapist would focus on building up the individual's self-esteem.

Freud and Freud's Influence

Sigmund Freud was born in 1856, and at a young age his family settled in Vienna where he lived for most of his life. He studied at the University of Vienna and received his MD in 1881. He was interested in psychiatry and over the next twenty years he would formulate, primarily through observations of his own case studies, his theories of psychoanalysis. His ideas were very influential through the first half of the 20th century and still have adherents today.

These theories focused mainly on the unconscious mind and repressed sexual memories and fantasies from childhood. He developed the method of talk therapy to try to get the patient to bring these unconscious thoughts to the surface. He posited that the mind was made up of three parts – the id, the superego, and the ego.

The id represents the instinctual, animalistic aspects of the psyche, including sexual desires, and operates on the pleasure principle – every desire should be fulfilled immediately. The superego consists of all the values and morals of society, the rules we have internalized. The ego is the conscious self that moderates between the demands of the id and the superego. The ego operates according to what was called 'the reality principle' – trying to meet the demands of the id, while facing the reality of the limitations of the self, the demands of society, and the moral rules of the superego.

Guilt enters the picture when the ego tries to satisfy the desires of the id, knowing that the moral rules of the superego are being violated. The superego then imposes guilt on the individual, essentially as a punishment for giving into the id. In Freud's view, the individual is trapped within this conflict, and can never completely resolve it. One can only do the best one can to mitigate these feelings through better understanding of oneself.

Though Freudian psychoanalysis is no longer dominant in the field of psychiatry, Freud's influence is still felt. Many of the important psychological theories of the last century owe a debt to Freud. Psychologists such as Carl Jung, Alfred Adler, Wilhelm Reich, Fritz Perls, Arthur Janov, and Erich Fromm created new theories of the psyche that expanded on Freud's ideas. Today psychotherapists and counselors often still follow a basic model of talk therapy aimed at bringing repressed memories to the surface.

Summary

As we have seen in this chapter, there are diverse ideas about guilt within the different religions, philosophies, and other thought and belief systems we have examined. What they all share in common is an awareness of guilt's existence and a set of rules or beliefs or tenets that the individual is supposed to live by in order to avoid feelings of guilt. This diversity is one of the challenges one faces when having to make any decisions in life, especially those that have some ethical or moral feature to them.

In the next chapter, we will explore how we form the rules and beliefs that will guide us in making those decisions, looking at all the different influences in our lives that aid in that formation. These are the rules whose violation leads to feelings of guilt, whether imposed externally on us or only experienced internally. Once we have looked closely at how these seemingly external influences affect us, we will, through understanding the

Course, turn the whole process upside down, realizing how we have created this external world.

Chapter 3

The Rules-Based Life

Having established our definition of guilt, we now want to explore a particular part of that definition – Where do we learn what is wrong? This will require us to discover the influences that lead us to shape our own personal world of beliefs about right and wrong.

By exploring those influences, we hope to make it easier to see how it is really what we believe that makes us take action in this world, and it is what we believe that leads us to feel guilty. In this chapter we will treat those influences as if they are coming from an 'external' world. Later we will discover through the Course that all of these influences are ultimately internal – in our minds.

Our Rules and Beliefs

Everyone experiences a different external world with influences coming from a myriad of different directions and different times. It would be impossible to discuss all these influences to fully describe everyone's experience. Instead we will follow the development of a hypothetical person using a simple chronology starting from birth and proceeding throughout the person's life. It is hoped that the reader will recognize many of these influences, even though the exact chronology may be different.

What is universal is the process of building a system of beliefs and rules throughout our lives, and it is these rules that provide the structure through which we experience the physical world. We refer to these rules, both consciously and subconsciously, as we make the decisions in our lives. We believe that without this set of rules, we would be adrift, unable to make clear decisions, unable to function in this world.

As we will see later, it is these very rules that prevent us from fully experiencing the peace and wonder of life. It is also the guilt we feel when we violate these rules that prevents us from seeing the love all around us.

Parents

So let us examine the life of our hypothetical person. To one's everyday self it appears as if life begins at birth. It seems we have entered this world with a blank slate, and everything we are and feel and believe, is the result of our experiences in this world. We will for now take this point of view, but later we will see how this is all the result of a great deception.

For almost everyone in this world, the first influencers are our parents. In the first few weeks of life, the parents' role is to attend to the needs of a helpless infant. Feeding, changing diapers, holding, caressing, all done out of love for the child to meet the basic needs of life. At this stage the child appears to be only focused on these needs and minimally involved in observing the world around him.

Eventually the child becomes more aware and more mobile, interacting with the world outside the body, and now the parent begins to take on a teaching role. At some point there will be the first declaration of the word 'No', and the child's learning process begins, as he tries to make sense of the first disapprovals of his actions. Through a process of reward and disapproval, a system of beliefs about right and wrong is transmitted from the parents to the child.

Our bodies come into this world to learn through experience – what is painful and what is pleasurable. To some extent it is the role of the parent to limit these experiences to ones that are not truly harmful. For example, if the child gets too close to a hot stove, the parent will forcefully tell the child to stay away, rather than letting him get burned in order to learn the rule of not touching a hot stove. Thus will begin the development of the child's internal rules through a combination of learning and direct experience.

As the child gets older, the parents will help the child learn to socialize with others. In the next section we will look at the influence of one's peers on the development of beliefs, but the earliest social interactions are often scripted by the parents. Eventually as the child moves through the pre-teen and teen years, the parents become less important in the formation of these rules, and in fact, the child may begin to reject the words of the parents, seeking to strike out more on his own.

This will often be the beginning of an active rebellion on the child's part. This rebellion will vary in degree, depending on the child's nature and on external circumstances. This rebellion is another key step in the process of individuation. The teenager wants to strike out on his own, and in so doing will develop his own internal set of rules, a combination now of multiple influences.

Once the child reaches his early 20s, the rebellion against the parental influence often fades, and he will begin his work life and may start a family. At this point the circle is complete as the child is now the parent of a new generation, and the process of inculcating beliefs will fall to this new parent. There will always be differences from generation to generation, but the process is essentially the same.

Peers

When a child first begins to play with other children, the parents will instruct him to be kind to others, to share, and in essence to behave in a way that will put the parents and the whole family group in a good light. But there will then be a new influence emerging as he learns directly from others of his own age. This process continues throughout life, and the beliefs and rules from the parents will be altered as they are applied to one's peers.

One's peers can be thought of as a web of relationships where each connection in the web is approximately equal. Ideas can enter the web at any point and from that point can spread to others nearby or to a much wider part of the web. For example, think of popular music or fashion, where the introduction of a new song or style can move through this web of peers at great speed. Any one person may learn about a new style from one friend, but that person learned about it from another friend, etc.

Because of the close interaction of peers and the sense that others in this group are equals and share similar beliefs and ideas, peer interactions run separate from interactions with one's parents or other authority figures. Often it is within peer groups where rebellion starts and plays out. New music, new styles, and radical ideas can be fostered within the peer group and can be seen as a counter to the rules the parents have tried to instill in the growing child.

As one enters adulthood, peers continue to play a central part in the establishment of the rules that govern our lives. Our friends usually share our ideas about the world, often coming from similar cultures and having similar spiritual and religious beliefs. Though we may find friendship with ones who seem very different from us, it is the similarities, wherever those may be found, that bond us together.

Once the bond is formed with our friends, we may listen to new ideas coming from these friends and through that process alter our beliefs about the world. We can examine these ideas and compare them to the rules we currently use, and consciously or subconsciously decide to change some of those rules. In evaluating these new ideas, we might decide to change from a pragmatic point of view or perhaps even from an aesthetic sense. In any case, the process of evaluating new ideas is a constant one throughout life, and our peers are a ready source for those ideas.

Society

Beyond the close relationships of family and friends is the influence of the larger society. Whether we consider one's neighborhood, one's community, one's country, or the planet as a whole, we can be influenced by ideas we learn through a wide variety of media and other information sources. Once these ideas are considered, we can make them our own and create new rules for ourselves.

In most modern societies, books, television, and the internet provide a vast array of news and entertainment sources. We can be influenced to change beliefs by the news we watch or the entertainment we consume. In the news we can listen to political arguments, we can see acts of violence and altruism, and we can learn about far away countries and how people there view us. All of these can potentially lead to changes in our internal rules.

Though entertainment may be thought of as a non-core experience, often the subtle messages coming through dramas and comedies and art and music can drive emotional experience that leads to changes in our internal rules. Sometimes as we become inured to the everyday news we see, a powerful artistic experience can lead us to re-examine some of our core beliefs.

For example, suppose you are a basically patriotic young person, believing that though the leaders of the country are not always right, it's important to support the actions of your country in the world. Suppose you then see a movie that shows in graphic detail the horrors of a war you thought very little about while living your everyday life. You might have to re-examine those patriotic beliefs in the light of your emotional experience.

This process will continue throughout life, just as the influences from parents, other family members, and peers will continue. The person you believe you are today has a very different set of beliefs than the person you were in the past, even though many of these changes in belief are very subtle and may not be obvious. We try to build a picture of ourselves as one solid, consistent self, but underneath it all, our beliefs and internal rules are in constant flux.

The Rules-Based Life

Religion and Philosophy

When it comes to the fundamental questions of life and death and our behavior in the world, religion and philosophy offer the strongest, most rigid set of beliefs. Even if one is a secularist eschewing religion for a materialist, scientific philosophy, there is a clearly defined set of rules for how one interacts with the world.

Throughout history, most societies have believed in a deity or deities of some sort, and through these beliefs established clear codes of behavior. In some of these religions, there are well-defined punishments for violations of these codes, and these punishments may occur in this life or be put off to some judgment time in the afterlife. There are also rewards for what is defined as 'good' behavior, perhaps a favored place in the residence of the deity.

In most of these cases, there has been some kind of revelatory process through which these rules were handed down, and in most cases this revelation comes to us from the distant past. Over the centuries, as society changes, these revelatory rules are re-interpreted to fit modern life. Some will insist on holding on to ancient practices while others may want to have a more direct experience of the deity. This often leads to conflict within the institution of the religion.

Different people will internalize these religious rules differently as well. For example, suppose there are two individuals sitting across the aisle from one another attending a Catholic Mass. The two are hearing the same words being spoken by the priest, they were taught the same Catholic teachings as they grew up, and they both attend Mass regularly.

But one may believe homosexuality is a sin and the other may not. One may believe that women should become priests and the other may not. One may believe the path to God is through regular confession to a priest followed by proper penitence, and the other may believe in a more direct experience and path to God.

The reality is that no matter how clear-cut religious rules are, everyone will have to interpret those rules within the context of everyday life. As mentioned previously, how do we deal with a prohibition on killing? Is all killing wrong, or do circumstances matter? Is the killing of a bug under foot as you walk along really a sin? If so, life could get very difficult. Is intention the difference in right or wrong killing? What about someone with mental health problems for whom intention is hard to determine? The questions can get very sticky.

What really happens is that we take all these seemingly rigid rules, along with our parental teaching, along with our peer and societal influences and form our very own set of internal beliefs. We may not even realize what rules we are operating under much of the time, but we will use them to decide what is wrong and therefore what we should feel guilty about.

Guilt and the Rules-Based Life

So now let's look at how we take these rules and apply them to our lives, and how through violating these rules we can experience guilt. Previously four examples were presented of individuals who had experiences that led them to feel guilty. Now we'll go through these and look at what internal rules were violated and how those rules were formed in each individual.

Example 1: Sarah is feeling guilty because she lost control of her anger and lashed out at her sister, and also because she feels she has failed to achieve success in life. There are two rules at work here, one reinforcing the other.

The first rule was formed in Sarah's mind at a very early age. Her parents instilled in her the belief that one should not show one's anger toward others. If you feel anger, it's important that you suppress it. This rule was strengthened during Sarah's school years as she learned to interact in a proper way with her peers. Her church added another level to the rule, making her failure to follow it not only a personal transgression, but a transgression against God and her church as well.

The second rule has to do with Sarah's beliefs about what it means to succeed in life. As she began to grow up, her parents started putting pressure on her to succeed, first in school, and later in the world of work and career. She had the example of her sister, who always did well at whatever she tried. She now feels inadequate and a failure, having been unable to live up to her parents' expectations. Now her sister embodies many of those same expectations. She feels guilty that she somehow should have done better.

Example 2: Michael's feelings of guilt stem from the affair he is having with a colleague at work. He also feels guilty about having to lie to his wife. He is violating an internal rule about fidelity in marriage and about honesty with someone you love.

His beliefs about relationships and marriage were first formed from observing his parents and other couples as he grew up. Most of this was unconscious, but as he watched these interactions, he began to form ideas about how one should behave within the context of a marriage. Fidelity seemed to be one of the most important requirements. This idea was reinforced by his church, to the point of making infidelity a significant sin.

As he grew older and learned more through the media and peers, he relaxed those ideas a bit, seeing that though infidelity was always a problem in a marriage, it was not always the end and was sometimes part of the transition to a new relationship. The old feelings from childhood, though, never completely went away, and no matter how he rationalized his new affair, the guilt was still very strong.

His feelings about honesty started at a very young age as his parents scolded him not to lie. He also learned later on through observation that lies in relationships usually create problems, and usually can't be maintained for any length of time. The truth will come out. He can't bring himself to be honest with his wife, but he feels guilty for not doing so.

Example 3: David is a hard-working husband and father, who has always had a loving relationship with his mother. When she gets cancer, and needs several years of care, he doesn't feel he can take his focus off of his wife, children, and job to care for her. The only option financially is to put her in a nursing home. He feels tremendous guilt about not doing more for her.

Our relationship with our parents starts from birth and lasts until they or we leave this world. There is no other relationship with such a bond and so many opportunities for love and conflict. Every religion in the world to some degree encourages us to honor our parents. We also often feel a debt to them, knowing they sacrificed in order to raise us.

David's guilt comes from that core place of loving and honoring his mother, but feeling unable to give her everything he feels he should. He knows that with all of his commitments, something had to lose out, and in this case it was his mother. He did what he felt he could to make her last days as comfortable as possible, but he could never feel he had done enough. The rule about honor toward our parents is a powerful one.

Example 4: Melissa makes a simple, momentary decision to drive when she knew she probably shouldn't. She didn't want to disappoint her friend and she felt they would be all right. Tragically Susan is killed and Melissa has to deal with the consequences.

Here the rules are about responsibility to others and to the law. As a young child the consequences of irresponsible behavior are usually relatively minor. We are scolded or must apologize to others. As we get older we begin to see that irresponsible behavior can have greater costs, and sometimes can lead to violations of the laws of our government.

Melissa was not acting responsibly toward Susan or possibly toward others who may have been on the road that night. She knew what she was doing was wrong and likely illegal, but it just didn't seem to be a big deal in the moment. Once the consequences of her action sunk in, guilt was inevitable, a guilt placed on her by society and a guilt felt deeply inside her.

The Course and Rules

So now we see how we form rules and beliefs in our lives and how we make decisions based on these rules. These rules will change throughout our lives as we take different paths and are influenced in different ways. If we were to write down all the rules and beliefs we have when we are 15 and then looked back on these at age 40, most likely we would be amazed how much our beliefs have changed, even though we feel like we are basically the same person.

At any point in our lives, when it comes time for a decision, we at least subconsciously refer to these rules to choose our plan of action. If, for whatever reason, we make a decision to violate a rule, we are likely to feel guilt, especially if our actions appear to cause some external harm. No matter how clearly we think we know what our internal rules are, we are at times unable to follow them. Sometimes emotions seem to be out of control, and we take action against our better judgment.

This is what everyday life looks like as we find ourselves as individuals experiencing life in the external physical world, a world of bodies and form and a great deal of pain and suffering and ultimately death. This world feels very real, this pain and guilt feels real, and death seems tragically real.

For the rest of this book, we will look at all of this from a different perspective, the perspective of the Course. We will see how this world that seems so real to us is actually an illusion, a complex mental construction with no true reality. We will see how we got to this point of believing in the illusion by accepting the idea of separation. We will see how the ego does everything in its power to maintain the illusion. And finally we will discover a way out of the illusion through the Course's brand of forgiveness.

In the next chapter, we will step aside from our focus on rules and beliefs and explore the basic philosophy of the Course. Next we will look in detail at how the Course views the concept of guilt. The antidote to guilt, forgiveness, will then be explored with practical examples. Finally we will look at what a world without guilt would look like.

Chapter 4

The Philosophy of *A Course in Miracles*

This chapter is a condensed version of my previous work, *It's All Mind: The Simplified Philosophy of A Course in Miracles*. It presents the basic philosophy of the Course so that we may use those concepts to examine how we can free ourselves from guilt through forgiveness.

The philosophy begins with some assumptions about the nature of God and the Natural State of Being. In this philosophy, the existence of God is unquestioned, though the God of the Course varies significantly from the God of most religions. Most importantly, this God is Mind and only Mind, and anything we believe that exists other than Mind is simply an illusion.

We will see how the idea of separation is a core concept, and how our belief in that separation has led us to believe we exist within a world external to ourselves. We will then learn how through forgiveness we can free ourselves of this illusion of separation and how we can move beyond the negative experience of our lives to re-experience our Natural State of Peace within a Loving God.

God

There is a quote from the Course, "We say 'God is,' and then we cease to speak..." (W-169.5). From a pure experience point of view, this is all that needs to be said. The True God of *A Course in Miracles* is Pure Oneness and cannot be described using our dualistic point of view and language. However, in order to understand the experience of our everyday world, the Course and this philosophy need to talk about God from a dualistic point of

43

view at times – describing what God is like and what God is not like.

There are many descriptive statements that might be made about God, but it will be sufficient for this development to consider the following four aspects of God.

1 - God is All That Is, Everything. There is nothing that is not God.

2 - God is Mind, Thoughts, Ideas and nothing but Mind.

3 - God is Pure Love. All experiences of God are Loving.

4 - God Creates. God is not static, but is in a constant state of Creating.

If there were complete acceptance and belief in these four aspects, there would be no need for the Course. The purpose of the Course is to help us discover the barriers that prevent us from believing these ideas and to teach us how to remove those barriers.

1 – God is All That Is, Everything

Rather than just being omnipresent, in this philosophy God *is* everything. Nothing exists outside of God. If we believe we are experiencing something that is not God, we are simply fooling ourselves. Specifically this means the belief we are bodies or souls living in this world, and God is an entity outside of us, is an illusion.

2 – God is Mind

One of the more radical concepts in this philosophy is that God is only Mind. The only true experiences are ideas in the Mind of God, and since only Mind is real, anything material, physical, corporeal, etc. must be an illusion. The entire physical world with all of its complexity is just an illusory thought, and if we believe something is solid, permanent, or objective, we are deluding ourselves. In this philosophy everything happens in our minds, and any change we want to see must take place in our minds.

3 – God is Pure Love

In our world it is difficult to imagine an experience of Pure Love, but it is fundamental to the philosophy that God is only Love. If we think we are experiencing a God that is in any way less than a Loving God, then that 'God' is another illusion. We will see how in this philosophy one of the barriers to the experience of God is to see a 'God' that is not Loving. A 'God' that is judgmental, punishing, or merely too remote and abstract to experience is not a Loving God and must be illusory.

4 – God Creates

It is important not to see God as a static experience. God is the Source of our being – our True Self is God's creation, and this creation takes place in the Mind of God, which is the only place it can happen. Once created, this Self is fundamentally a co-creator extending the experience of God. Those creations occur in the Mind of God and therefore only exist and are only experienced in the Mind of God.

So why do we experience in our everyday lives something so different from this Natural State of Being? How is it possible we experience something other than Love? How can we possibly experience pain and attack or guilt and fear? All of these can be traced to our belief in the idea of separation.

The Idea of Separation

Having described the four aspects of God, we are now looking for a logical development that will lead us to better understand how we got to our current state of being from our Natural State. It is only necessary to find a single such development that can describe our current experience. The key fact is all of this is taking place within the mind, which allows for great freedom.

Suppose for a moment there was a thought of being separate from God. If the Mind of God *is* Everything, how can the thought of being separate from God exist? Since God is Creative, any thoughts are possible and free to be explored, so in some small corner, the illusory thought of separation is possible. But can a part of God's Mind actually separate from the Mind of God? In reality it cannot, but that does not mean the idea of separation and all of the possibilities it would entail cannot be explored. This is where we find ourselves.

Once the thought of separation occurs, the next question is, How would such a separation manifest itself and what would the experience be like? The first realization is that in order for any part of God to believe it has separated from God, it must delude itself, since real separation is impossible. How might such a delusion be formed?

Denying God

First the experience of God would have to be avoided, since this experience would break the spell of the belief in separation. One way to do this would be to introduce the idea of fear and the idea of something to be feared. In this scenario, God would become the focus of the fear; for if we do not fear God and were to re-experience the God of Pure Love, the illusion of separation would fall apart.

One way to create a fear of God is to see this new 'God' as an enemy who is out to harm us in some way, perhaps by judging us and potentially wanting to punish us for what we have done. This may sound preposterous, since God, by definition, is Pure Love, but it shows how absurd the idea of separation is and how much must be done to prop it up. If God were considered a friendly presence, the attraction to re-experience the Loving God would be too strong.

The Separated Self

So an illusion has been created that essentially creates a ring around a portion of those thoughts of separation. Within that ring, all the thoughts are focused on seeing what is outside the ring as dangerous and fearful – an enemy. To reiterate, the ring, the fear, the enemy, are all imagined and have no basis in truth, and they can only maintain their illusory state by constant effort to see something that is not there. The thoughts within that ring we will call the separated self.

Now suppose this scenario has been played out and a new separated self has been created. Of course, there really is no separated self, but there is a belief it has been created. This self will live in a state of fear, loneliness, and guilt for having cut itself off from what was its Natural Loving State of Being.

This state creates a great tension between the misery of the separated state and the nearness of God. The separated self will want to distance itself from this misery by building new barriers, new thoughts and ideas to focus on that will help it forget its true Natural State. One way the self can do this is to create within the ring the illusion of a separate external world, onto which it can project all of its guilt, pain, and fear.

The Separate External World

This external world is another construct of ideas, but the separated self can now believe it is real, a place where the self sees attacks occurring, along with pain and fear. Of course, all of this pain is being projected by the self onto the world, and then being perceived as external to the self.

At this point the separated self can create the illusion of countless other separated selves, all existing in this projected world, and all interacting with one another, all projecting their thoughts out onto the world. The self can now be free of responsibility for the original thought of separation and allow the blame to be externalized. This has the additional benefit of creating a further layer of separation from God and the experience of Love.

The separated self can see itself as a lone bit of sanity in an insane external world – a world where the experience of love is fleeting, where death is always waiting, where attack, whether physical or emotional, is always present. By focusing on this world and learning how to defend itself from all these attacks, the memory of the Natural State fades further away. Of course, all of this is one great illusion, but the separated self will do what it must to maintain the idea of separation.

Since the separated self has created the external world to be a place of fear and attack, whenever this self interacts with this world, it will experience exactly what it projects onto that world. As the self further learns to project and then interact with the world, it begins to see the external world as its home. It becomes dependent on that world for its life and its sustenance. It begins to build up defenses to the attacks that are, by definition, part of that world – the world that is a completely delusional projection.

When discussing this separated self, it is important to understand that this self does not represent a person or a soul or any other of our common ideas of what a self is. Here the separated self is simply a construct of illusions that created the ring that separates these thoughts from the Oneness of the true Mind of God. The ring is not real and the idea of a separated self that can experience pain and guilt and fear is not real. But for the separated self, the illusion seems real, the external world seems real, and the pain and guilt and fear seem real.

For the remainder of the discussion, we will refer to the part of the separated self that focuses on maintaining the separation as the 'ego'. Later we will find there is another part of this separated self still connected to its Source that offers an alternative to the ego.

The Ego

The ego is the part of the separated self that focuses solely on the maintenance of the belief in separation. So what methods might the ego use to further the sense of separation and aloneness of the separated self? Most importantly, the ego must use whatever it can, especially guilt and fear, to prevent the separated self from remembering its connection to God. One of the ways it can maintain this belief is to try to keep the separated self focused on a separate external world.

The Philosophy of *A Course in Miracles*

The External World

We have talked about the concept of the separated self and discussed the fact that there is no self that was created, but only a construct of ideas. One of the ego's goals is to create a solid feeling of self, of being an isolated individual living in an external objective world. The external world we experience is a projection of the ego. The ego imagines guilt, fear, and attack and then creates a complete external world that contains all of the same guilt, fear, and attack.

The self then perceives this world as external and must use its focus and energies interacting with this world as if it was completely separate, when in reality it is all its own projection. The people we interact with, nature in all of its power and uncertainty, our activities, jobs, and creative work are all part of this ego construction. In order to interact with this projected world, the ego takes it one step further and constructs and maintains the illusion of a body.

The Body

As part of this illusion the ego creates a body with a precise sense of inside and outside. Within the body we appear to be at the mercy of our internal metabolic processes while from outside the body we are at the mercy of external forces. We spend, at the ego's request, a tremendous amount of our time building up defenses for our bodies. We build houses and other spaces to live, work, and play in. We procure and prepare sustenance for our bodies. The goal is to prolong the body in what we define (really what the ego defines) as a healthy state.

But lurking in our future is some kind of sickness, and that sickness may be generated internally in the body or it may be the result of some external agent that causes the sickness. Once we are sick, we must find external solutions to combat the sickness, and the ego tells us if we just take the right medicine or have the particular surgery or other procedure, we can return our bodies to health. But when we are old or too sick to keep our bodies going, we believe death will be the final chapter.

49

The Idea of Death

The ego has created an even greater idea to focus the energies of the self away from God – the idea of death. Everyone learns from an early age that their bodies and other bodies are all going to die eventually. Our societies exert great effort and resources to prolong the life of the body to put off death as long as possible. But we also know death could occur in the next instant, and therefore we as bodies are never secure in this world. Given that experience, how could we imagine there was a Loving God who put us and our bodies in this world?

Then what is death? The answer lies in understanding what it is that is dying. When we examine human death, the only thing we are sure is dying is the human body. But the body is a creation of the ego, which is a part of the separated self. So the death of a body is only the death of an illusion – an illusion the ego has created to try to trap the separated self in this external world. In our philosophy, the Mind of God is eternal and the Mind of God is Everything, so no matter how compelling it may seem, death is just another illusion created by the ego.

Hiding From God

As was mentioned, it is essential to the ego that we do not re-experience our existence within the Mind of God. God must be feared and we must feel deep guilt about our fear of God. There are basically two belief systems that exist in our world. One denies the existence of God, and for those who believe this, the world is a place of chance and chaos. One never knows what nature may inflict upon the self in this world – earthquakes, job loss, a car accident, loss of a friend, or perhaps the asteroid that hits the earth. This means the self must be in a constant state of fear. The fear may be deeply hidden and the external personality may be bright, but the ego-driven actions the self takes will be centered on how to maintain the body in this uncertain world.

The second basic belief, which pervades almost all religions to some extent, is the idea of God as a judgmental entity. In this scenario there is usually a concept of a life after death, and what that life is like is a result of what we do while we are here. Once again the ego creates a 'God' that is not Pure Love and we must be in fear of that 'God' because our future is in its hands. Since we can never live the life completely that we are told we should (told by the ego, of course), we are constantly feeling guilty knowing we are offending this 'God'.

In both of these scenarios, the True God is hidden, and the fact this whole construction is a total illusion is obscured. If we can just go back to before the separation, there was and is nothing but the Mind of God, and all of the ego's manipulations are focused on maintaining the forgetting. As we will see later, there are ways to start to remember who and what we really are, ways that will ignore what the ego tells us is true and allow us to begin to see what is really there.

Judgment

Another tool the ego uses to focus the separated self on the external world is judgment. When we see this world from the ego's dualistic point of view, we are constantly judging the experiences, people, and ideas of this world. Fundamentally everything is looked at as to whether it increases pain or pleasure, and the mere process of judging means we have accepted the dualism of the ego. Thus judgment helps to perpetuate the ego.

There are two fundamental lessons the Course tries to teach us. The first is to recognize how the ego operates in our lives as it projects onto the world all of our internal guilt, fear, and pain. In recognizing the actions of the ego, we begin to see the barriers that prevent us from experiencing the Love of God. The second lesson is to learn how to break through those barriers through the practice of forgiveness.

Forgiveness

In this development we started with the four aspects of God. We then explored how a world like our current experience might have evolved, which led to the concept of separation, a mental construct of illusory ideas. We defined that ringed off set of ideas as the separated self, and the ego as the portion of the separated self focused on maintaining the separation. We examined how the ego creates the illusion of our separate external world, with our bodies inhabiting that world, and the many ways the ego maintains the illusion.

We now want to look at the part of the separated self that remembers the Natural State within the Mind of God. The ego wants to suppress that memory any way it can, but the memory is there nonetheless. The Course offers us the idea of forgiveness as our way to break the hold of the ego and to let the memory come to the surface. By forgiving the world we perceive, we will begin the journey back to God.

What Is Forgiveness?

In common usage forgiveness means to give up resentment toward someone or something. The word is used often in Christian thought, but can also be used as a psychological term. In either case the resentment is seen as detrimental, and forgiveness will free us from those feelings. The term is most often used in regard to forgiving another person for some attack on oneself, whether physical, psychological, or emotional. In any case the assumption is the attack did occur and you are simply letting go of your resentment toward the person who attacked you.

In the Course, forgiveness has a very different and specific meaning and a unique power. Remember we began with our True Existence in the Mind of God. All else is illusion, including the separated self and the world in which that self believes it is living. If this is all an illusion then any attack on this self must be an illusion as well. The ego wants us to see the attack as real, but if we can realize it is an illusion, the attack has no power against the self. This is what is meant by forgiveness in the Course – realizing the attack never really happened. In essence we forgive our perception of the event, which by extension forgives the person as well. The ego has projected the world we perceive, so as we forgive the world around us, we weaken the power of the ego.

No Degrees of Attack

It is important to realize the word attack is used in a very general sense and there are no degrees of attack. Being physically attacked is just the same as someone saying an unkind word about you, or a politician wanting to raise your taxes or take away your benefits, or your boss demanding something from you. In all these cases the ego has projected an experience that is not perceived as loving, and in all these cases forgiveness can free your perception of the experience and allow you to realize the ego was fooling you again. It doesn't matter where you begin your forgiveness, it only matters that you apply it to everything. If you withhold forgiveness for any one thing, the ego has maintained its illusion of separation.

The Holy Spirit

Of course it's not always going to be easy to forgive. The mere fact we perceive ourselves as bodies living in an external world means we have given a great deal of power to the ego, whose sole reason for being is to maintain the separation. We said earlier there is another part of the separated self that remembers the Mind of God. The Course refers to this part as the Holy Spirit.

The term Holy Spirit clearly has a Christian origin, but as with many ideas in the Course, the definition is very different. It really makes no difference what we call this part of the separated self – the Self That Remembers, the Inner Voice, the Inner Guide – what is important is the meaning.

The Holy Spirit and Forgiveness

The Holy Spirit might be seen within our minds as a personality or a larger than life spiritual entity. We envision this entity as being the part that remembers our True Existence. The process of forgiving an attack starts with recognizing we have perceived an attack occurring in the external world. We then take that attack, and knowing that to the Holy Spirit the attack could never have occurred, we hand off to the Holy Spirit all of our feelings about the attack, and by doing so we free ourselves of these feelings.

A more visual and less personal way to think of the Holy Spirit is as a tunnel that opens out from the ego's world through the ego's barriers and through the outer ring into the True Mind of God. It's a mental path through which we access our Natural State. By envisioning this tunnel we can again hand off the pain, guilt, and fear that we experience in the ego's world, so it can be sucked into that tunnel to disappear into the Mind of God. What is happening when we do this is we are for a brief moment remembering where we came from, and by doing so we are forgiving the experience which led to our feelings of attack.

What Else Can We Forgive?

We have been focusing on forgiveness in the context of forgiving another person for a perceived attack. When we use the method of forgiveness from the Course, we are really forgiving the experience of the attack. By extension the person who we believed attacked us in the first place is also forgiven, since if the attack did not occur, the person did not commit the attack.

We can extend this idea of forgiveness to internal guilt about acts we believe we have committed in the past, illnesses that may appear to have come from within the body or from an outside agent, the fears we have about attacks that could occur in the future, and our judgments and the judgments of others. And of course there is also the fear and guilt we feel about our initial rejection of the Loving God and our replacement with the ego's concept of the judgmental 'God' or the non-existent God.

Guilt and Fear of God

Some of the deepest fear and guilt we experience are related to our feelings about God. Remember the whole idea of separation started with our rejection of the Loving God and the creation of a judgmental, punishing 'God', or the belief there is no God. In either case we have substituted the Loving place in the Mind of God with a non-Loving experience in this world, which has led to deep pain, guilt, and fear. We must forgive our guilt for believing we left God and our fear of some kind of retribution from the judgmental 'God'. The Holy Spirit stands ready to help us heal those feelings as well. First we must recognize our part in creating this illusion and then release those feelings to the Holy Spirit to remember again our Existence in the Loving Mind of God.

The Way Home

We began our philosophy with the four aspects of God. These aspects define our Natural State of Being. Then the idea of separation occurred, which is just an illusion, but the idea led to the ringed off separated self, another illusion. We defined the ego as the part of the separated self that maintains the illusion of separation. We explored the different ways the ego works to maintain that illusion. We then learned about forgiveness and how through forgiveness we can begin to break the hold of the ego. With the help of the Holy Spirit, the part of the separated self that remembers its Natural State, we free ourselves of the pain, guilt, and fear in our lives.

The first part of the development of the philosophy is focused on understanding how we got where we are and how we maintain our current separated state. Through this understanding we can begin to recognize the actions of the ego. Once recognition has occurred, we begin to forgive all the attacks at all different levels in our lives. Through this process of forgiveness, we are letting go, step by step, of the separation illusion, and we will remember more and more our Natural Existence in the Mind of God.

Peace

So where does all of this lead? The stated goal in the Course is to experience Peace. What does Peace mean in the Course? In essence it is a state of continual forgiveness, living your life with a constant realization the world we inhabit is an illusion and is not our True Home. As events occur, they are instantly seen as illusions, instantly forgiven, and any negative feelings are passed on to the Holy Spirit. By continually forgiving our experiences in this world, the ego is no longer in charge of the separated self. The pain, guilt, and fear that are normally experienced are forgiven and this new self identifies more and more with the Holy Spirit. The remembrance of the True Natural State becomes ever stronger.

How can we experience this Peace? As with many things we learn in this world, through constant practice. The ego is a strong force and before coming to the Course we spent much of our lives believing the ego's view of the world, a place of fear and attack from which we must protect ourselves. Once we open ourselves to an awareness of the Holy Spirit's presence, we can begin the process of breaking down all of the ego's barriers – all of the guilt and fear we have accepted from the ego throughout our lives.

Through the experience of the Holy Spirit, we can begin to remember on a daily basis our True Existence in the Mind of God. Eventually that daily remembrance can become a constant remembrance and a state of continual forgiveness can be achieved. Peace can be ours whether our bodies continue to inhabit this world or not. Once forgiveness is a constant practice, and Peace becomes our everyday experience, there is nothing in the world that can take this from us. Our Peace is our own and any attack on that Peace is just a fleeting illusion that will instantly die away.

The End of Illusion

There will come a time when this world of illusion and separation will be gone. Everything we currently experience – past, present, and future – will disappear. Once we find our way back to the Loving Mind of God, all of the illusions that have grabbed our focus will fade away. The separated self and the ring that encloses it, the ego and all of its tricks, our external world and all of the bodies in that world, even the Holy Spirit who helped lead us out of the illusion – all of these will be gone and we will live in a state of Love and Peace unimaginable to us where we are now.

Chapter 5

Guilt and *A Course in Miracles*

With this new philosophy in mind, we now focus on how the Course is applied to the idea of guilt. We will first examine where this guilt originally came from. Then we will look at examples of ways the ego uses guilt to try to keep us focused on the illusion of separation and how destructive those feelings of guilt can be in our everyday lives.

The Origin of Guilt

To understand where guilt comes from, we have to go back to the beginning. We need to look closely at that first moment when the idea of separation occurred, the moment we began to believe in this idea, the moment we began to fear and feel guilty. In that first moment, the separation idea itself looked back at God and created the illusion of fear and guilt in order to counter God's incredible Love.

This illusion took on a life of its own and layer upon layer of fear and guilt and attack and pain were built up to pull us further and further from knowledge of the True God. There was no other way to maintain the separation, and out of this grew the ego, the great maintainer. The ego will do whatever is possible to reinforce in us the belief that we must fear God and must feel guilty about the separation.

If the ego is the symbol of the separation, it is also the symbol of guilt. Guilt is more than merely not of God. It is the symbol of attack on God... This is the belief from which all guilt really stems (T-5.V.2).

We might call this guilt the original guilt. The ego has created so many other layers of guilt and fear on top of this original guilt that we seldom feel it directly anymore. But whether we feel it directly or not, every instance of guilt that we experience is merely a reflection of that original guilt. For if mind is all there is, everything we experience in this world is a projection of our minds, and every event that causes us fear or guilt is a projection as well. And underneath all these projections, it is ultimately our separation from God we feel guilty about.

No matter what our current attitude is about God, this original guilt is fundamental. If we believe that God doesn't exist and the material world we inhabit is simply the result of physical laws and processes, this is just another illusion, another layer of misdirection, given to us by the ego. If we believe in a 'God' that is in any way other than Pure Love, a 'God' who wants to judge us or punish us in any way, this is just one more illusion the ego presents us. As we state in the beginning of the philosophy, there is only one Mind in a state of Pure Love, and that is the only reality.

So as we discover those places in our lives where we feel guilty, and as we forgive each of those instances of guilt, we will be peeling back the layers of illusion the ego has created and we will be getting closer to seeing that original guilt. This will bring us right to the threshold of experiencing God again. But in order to get there, we must first see how the ego uses guilt in our everyday lives, discover where guilt exists within us, and find the path to releasing our guilt.

The Ego and Guilt

We will now look at how the ego builds up the layers of guilt and fear to prevent us from seeing the original guilt. We'll explore some of the methods the ego uses to induce guilt in us, and look at how we then project that guilt outward onto others to try to lift the burden on ourselves.

The continuing decision to remain separated is the only possible reason for continuing guilt feelings (T-5.V.8).

Guilt and *A Course in Miracles*

Remember the ego has only one purpose – to maintain the idea of separation. Everything the ego does is done to further this purpose, and guilt is its most powerful tool. Whether it's trying to keep us focused on our own guilt or it's showing us all the guilt in the external world, it uses guilt to keep us separated. This is the key to understanding the workings of the ego.

If you identify with the ego, you must perceive yourself as guilty. Whenever you respond to your ego you will experience guilt, and you will fear punishment (T-5.V.3).

We worry that some punishment, no matter how uncertain and vague, is lurking out there in the future. In relationships we worry someone might not want to be friends with us anymore if we're guilty of something. In religion, there seem to be negative consequences waiting for us if we make the wrong choice. The ego wants us to worry and to see these punishments, knowing that as long as we do, we will continue our guilt and continue to believe in the separation.

This is all based on that original guilt we felt when we rejected the True God and chose the idea of separation. In order to maintain our lives in their current state, we have to perpetuate this guilt, and in fact, the Course talks extensively about the attraction of guilt. When we're first presented with the idea that we would somehow be attracted to guilt, it seems absurd, but on more careful examination it makes perfect sense as long as we want to keep this illusion going.

Guilt is the only need the ego has, and as long as you identify with it, guilt will remain attractive to you (T-15.VII.10).

Guilt keeps us tied to this world, this illusion we call home. If you feel guilty about something you did, you will feel cut off from others, separated. If you see someone in the world who you believe is guilty, you will feel separate from that person. In either case, you are choosing the ego's view of the world, and in either case you are actively rejecting God.

If this guilt continues for any length of time, it is because you are attracted to it and are maintaining it, not because it is forced on you. The Course says, "[You] need do nothing except not to interfere" (T-16.I.3). When you are feeling guilty, you are interfering by actively keeping the guilt going because you are attracted to it more than you are attracted to your desire to remember God.

If you want to be free of the idea of separation, free of the ego, you must begin to free yourself from guilt. The first step is what you are doing now, seeing the process by which we all choose guilt. The next step it to personalize it, and look within yourself at how you are attracted to guilt and how you project guilt onto others. One place to discover this is through your anger.

All anger is nothing more than an attempt to make someone feel guilty... (T-15.VII.10).

This passage is crystal clear – anger is only justified if your goal is to induce guilt on another. In some schools of modern psychology, and even in some religions, anger can be seen as a healthy emotion if it doesn't get out of control. There are some schools of thought that tell us it is better to express our anger than to hold it in, and through that release we can achieve an emotional catharsis.

The Course says that's all bunk. If you feel anger toward anyone or any situation, whether you express it or not, your goal is to make someone or something guilty. There's no other explanation. You must learn to recognize why you are feeling angry. It has nothing to do with what is going on outside of you, but is instead a primary means to project your feelings of guilt outward.

Beware of the temptation to perceive yourself unfairly treated... Can innocence be purchased by the giving of your guilt to someone else? And is it innocence that your attack on him attempts to get? Is it not retribution for your own attack upon [another] you seek? Is it not safer to believe that you are innocent of this, and victimized despite your innocence? Whatever way the game of guilt is played, there must be loss. Someone must lose his innocence that someone else can take it from him, making it his own (T-26.X.4).

In trying to make someone else guilty, we are trying to take his innocence from him. We believe we will gain some new innocence by projecting our guilt outward. The reality is that this false innocence we may momentarily feel never lasts since we haven't really lost our guilt. We have just focused it outside ourselves in the hope this will somehow release us. The release will never come through projecting our guilt, it will only come through recognizing our own guilt and freeing it through forgiveness.

This whole process also affects our sense of time. The Mind of God is eternal, but as we travel through our illusory world, we seem to tick off the seconds leaving behind our past and moving into an unknown future that we know will ultimately lead to death.

Guilt feelings are the preservers of time. They induce fears of retaliation or abandonment, and thus ensure that the future will be like the past. This is the ego's continuity (T-5.VI.2).

So our sense of time is a direct result of the ego's use of guilt. By focusing us on past transgressions, whether ours or someone else's, we become fixated on that past. We then will worry about what kind of punishment we might receive or mete out in the future, and by so doing, we forget about the eternal present we all really live in and see only the failed past and the fearful, uncertain future. Without guilt, time would fall away as would all the ego's plans for us. With guilt, we see only this illusion, surrendering to the ego and the idea of separation our right to choose the eternal God.

When we look at the world as presented to us by the ego, it can all seem hopeless, as we are locked into a cycle of guilt and retribution that we're unable to escape. This is exactly the way the ego wants us to feel, for if we didn't, the idea of separation could not be maintained. In the next chapter we will examine how to apply forgiveness to guilt with the help of the Holy Spirit, and see that this sense of hopelessness has a cure.

The Ego and the Rules-Based Life

Yet consider how strange a solution the ego's arrangement is. You project guilt to get rid of it, but you are actually merely concealing it. You do experience the guilt, but you have no idea why. On the contrary, you associate it with a weird assortment of "ego ideals," which the ego claims you have failed (T-13.II.2).

Those "ego ideals" are the rules and beliefs you use to judge your behavior and the behavior of others. You believe they came from your interaction with the outside world, from your parents, your peers, society, and from religious and philosophical sources. It seems as if you travel through this world interacting with all these forces around you, when in reality this is all a projection of the ego.

Before we can make any progress on the return road to God, we must first recognize how the ego plan works, how we are constantly fooled by the ego into believing in what's not really there. Once we see this plan, we can begin the process of forgiveness that will free us from the ego's hold. Until we see the ego and all its rules and judgments for what they really are, we cannot go Home.

Now let's look at the different influences we discussed in the chapter on rules-based living. We started with our parents, who begin the process of instilling in us the norms of behavior. We appear to come into this world as a helpless being, and certainly from the point of view of this world, we could not survive here without the help of others.

It also seems as if we are mostly a blank slate, with only basic instinctual decision-making capability, such as how to feed and how to complain when we're uncomfortable. It seems as if it's up to our parents and others around us to teach us how to function in this world, which ultimately means how to behave in this world.

But what is really happening here? We are actually deciding moment by moment to listen to the ego, to look at the world around us through its eyes. We are choosing the ego's projections over our inner connection to the Holy Spirit. When our parents tell us we should do something a certain way or else there will be a punishment, we don't hear the ego's voice. We believe it is coming from outside of us.

Only if a child is taught from an early age that its true power comes from within and the world it sees outside itself is a projected illusion, can the ego's power be checked. Only if the child learns along with the basic needs of functioning in this world how to forgive this illusion, will he experience any kind of true happiness. And only if the child finds the Holy Spirit within will it be able to choose to reject the ego and its projections.

In a similar way, we need to examine our peer interactions, the learning that comes from those around us who are most like us in age and experience. Because of these similarities, we put great store in what we learn from peers. But each of these individuals sees an ego-projected world as well, and each of them experiences influences from others as well. We must recognize when these peers are acting in an ego-inspired way and not through the Holy Spirit. When we see it, we must be willing to forgive what we see.

Beyond the world of friends and family, there are the influences from the wider society we seem to live in, through the media, through religious teaching and ceremony, and through the education we receive. These influences have a different power, because we see that in this case it's not just those close to us, but perhaps millions of others who believe a certain way. We think there must be something to all this if these ideas have been around for centuries and much of the world believes in them.

In reality the length of time a rule or belief has existed, or the number of people who believe in it, has absolutely nothing to do with its truth. We can only see Truth within. What is projected outside of us is always of the ego and is always illusion. If we are not choosing for the Holy Spirit, we are choosing for the ego and the world we see will be full of judgment and fear and guilt. Forgiveness is the only release.

So ultimately all those rules and beliefs we have accumulated along the way, all those "ego ideals", whose violation leads to feelings of guilt, all are illusions we need to forgive. We must learn to recognize these ego-created rules within ourselves and one by one learn to forgive them. Feelings of guilt can lead us to this recognition if we allow the Holy Spirit to be our guide. In the next chapter we will focus on how to forgive the external world, the guilt, and the underlying rules at the heart of it all.

Examples of Guilt and the Ego

In this section, we will revisit our four examples of guilt and discover how these can be seen differently in light of our understanding of the ego and the ego's motivations.

Example 1: As we saw earlier, Sarah is feeling guilty because she lost control of her anger and lashed out at her sister, and also because she feels she has failed to achieve success in life. In our last look at Sarah's guilt, we pointed out that she felt she was violating two internal rules – the first that she should never show anger toward another person and the second concerning her belief in being a failure at life.

It's interesting to note that her first rule does not say she should never be angry, only that she should never express it outwardly. This is a classic ego ploy – allowing us to feel strong emotions, but not allowing us to express them. As we discussed above, Sarah's feelings of anger are the ego's attempt to make another person feel guilty, in this case her sister. Sarah is feeling wronged by her sister, and she is using this anger to project her own guilt onto another.

Another ego ploy is to never let us be completely happy about anything concerning the external world. It does this so that we can continue to be focused on the fear, guilt, and pain we see in this world. Sarah's beliefs about failure are the ego's way of convincing her she will never find happiness in this world. Sarah feels she has let others down by not living up to their expectations, and in doing so, she is letting the ego define who she should be in this world.

Example 2: Michael is feeling guilty about the affair he is having with a colleague at work. He is also feeling guilty about having to lie to his wife. He is violating his own internal rules about fidelity in marriage and about honesty with someone you love.

There is a concept in the Course of 'special relationships'. These are broadly categorized into special love and special hate relationships. In Michael's case we are looking at the special love relationship he has with his wife. In simplest terms, special love is conditional love, loving someone as long as some conditions are met and being loved as long as you satisfy certain conditions. True Love, the Love of God, is always unconditional, and though there may be a mix of conditional and unconditional love in a relationship, as long as there are some conditions, the ego is in charge.

Here Michael feels there is something lacking in his marriage. He's not getting what he believes he wants from his wife, and therefore he feels comfortable looking outside the marriage to meet those needs. It doesn't matter what specific needs these are, what matters is that these are conditions he has put on the relationship with his wife, this special love relationship, this ego-induced relationship, and he believes his wife is failing to meet those conditions.

Michael believes that if the conditions are not met, he can violate the rules of his marriage, but at the same time, he feels there is something wrong about it and he feels guilty. A classic ego move again – provide us with the temptation and the justification for acting, and then make us guilty for proceeding. To hide all of this, he must also lie to his wife, adding to the layers of guilt.

Example 3: David is feeling guilty about not having done enough for his dying mother. He has a great many responsibilities in his life – work, wife, children – and he doesn't believe he has the time and financial resources to satisfy everyone.

It is very common for parents to induce guilt in their children in order to affect their behavior. This can start from a very early age and this guilt can become deeply internalized in a child as he grows up. Then whether the parent tries to induce guilt or not, the child may automatically feel guilty in relating to the parents. Even if David's mother says nothing to him about her care, and thanks him along the way, he can create his own guilt simply by believing there was something more he could do.

The ego has set this all up. David's mother's guilt-inducing behavior perpetuates from one generation to the next the need for guilt. David's internalization of this guilt perpetuates guilt for David to pass to his children. Only if someone along the way sees how the ego creates the guilt, will there be an end to this cycle.

To the extent that David's relationship with his mother involves guilt, it is also a special love relationship. If the love between them was unconditional, then whatever he did and whatever she did, would be ok. This is the essence of True Love – whatever happens is ok, for this world is an illusion and when we realize this, the guilt and pain of our relationships will fall away.

Example 4: Melissa decides to drive her friend, Susan, home from a party, knowing she has had too much to drink. The tragic conclusion results in a wave of guilt – from Susan's family, from the community, from the legal system, and Melissa's own internal guilt.

When guilt reaches the level of the violation of a law of society, the commission of a crime, we tend to look more seriously on the offense and the associated guilt. But legal guilt is no less a projection of the ego than other types of guilt. The whole concept of the "ego ideals" is that there is a set of rules we must adhere to or else there will be some kind of punishment. The punishment may vary from simple discomfort to incarceration, but the concept is the same.

Susan's family will impose guilt onto Melissa, believing her irresponsibility has caused them great pain. The judge and jury will impose guilt on her, referencing specific laws she violated. And Melissa will impose guilt on herself, knowing she has violated internal rules about responsible behavior and caring for a friend.

The ego loves all of this. Everyone in this drama is projecting his or her own guilt onto the situation, increasing the pain and guilt of everyone else. The whole experience creates layer upon layer of increasing separation, the ultimate purpose of the ego. Love is nowhere to be found, and until someone breaks this chain of guilt, Love will remain hidden.

The ego is doing everything it can to pursue its mission of maintaining the idea of separation. As we choose the ego's path, we can only see ourselves and others as guilty and we will be constantly reminded of the fear and pain of the world we live in.

> Time seems to go in one direction, but when you reach its end it will roll up like a long carpet spread along the past behind you, and will disappear. As long as you believe [you and others are] guilty you will walk along this carpet, believing that it leads to death. And the journey will seem long and cruel and senseless, for so it is (T-13.I.3).

Now that we understand the ego better, let's see how we can free ourselves through forgiveness from all this senselessness and return to our True Home within the Mind of God.

For further study in the Course on how the ego uses guilt, refer to Chapter 5, Section V, "The Ego's Use of Guilt" and Chapter 19, Section IV, Part A-i, "The Attraction of Guilt".

Chapter 6

Releasing Our Guilt through Forgiveness

So far we have been focused on understanding this world we live in, this life we live, with all the guilt and fear and pain we see and experience. We have seen how throughout our history, guilt has played an essential role in defining who we believe we are. We have looked at how the ego uses our internal rules to keep us focused on the guilt we see in the world and within. And we have explored examples of individuals dealing with guilt and how the ego does all it can to perpetuate it.

Now it's time to walk in the other direction, away from building further layers of guilt at the ego's bidding. We are going to see how we can take control and begin to rip those layers off one by one through the practice of forgiveness. We will follow a steady path leading us back to the original guilt and ultimately to the remembrance of our True Home in the Mind of God.

What Forgiveness Is Not

In Chapter 4 we learned of the unique perspective the Course offers us on forgiveness. In this chapter we will explore the idea of forgiveness in more depth, focusing especially on applying forgiveness to the concept of guilt. We will begin by looking at what forgiveness is not.

As part of the history of guilt in Chapter 2, we discussed the common approach to forgiveness which is used in several religions and philosophies and often in modern psychology. In one form of this approach, one first recognizes he has been the victim of an attack from another. This attack can be verbal, an emotional slight, or a physical attack. It doesn't matter what the form is, it only matters that one person feels he has been wronged.

Once someone feels wronged, the religions, philosophies, or the psychologists tell the person it's important for him to forgive whoever attacked him. In some cases there is a clear series of steps that this forgiveness should take, which might include a direct communication to the individual of the intention to forgive. In a religious context, the forgiving person might also ask God to forgive the other person as well.

In the second form of this common forgiveness, someone feels he has wronged another person and is seeking forgiveness for himself. This might include apologizing to the other person, and perhaps offering some penance, monetary or otherwise. Again in a religious context, asking God for forgiveness may be a final step.

From the Course point of view, the problem with this approach is that in both cases, the person believes a real attack has occurred, either from another or toward another. The Course says all such attacks are illusions and therefore not real. If the person sees them as real, true forgiveness cannot occur.

> The ego, too, has a plan of forgiveness because you are asking for one, though not of the right teacher... The ego's plan is to have you see error clearly first, and then overlook it. Yet how can you overlook what you have made real? By seeing it clearly, you have made it real and cannot overlook it (T-9.IV.4).

The only conclusion is that this form of forgiveness is just another ploy of the ego, another way to keep you trapped in the idea of separation. The attack, if it is seen as real, increases the separation you feel between yourself and another person. Because you have followed the tenets of your religion or philosophy or therapist, you might feel you are further on the path to being a better person. The Course says this is all a meaningless exercise.

Forgiveness is an empty gesture unless it entails correction. Without this it is essentially judgmental, rather than healing (T-2.V.A.15).

In the next section we will discover how true forgiveness works, but for now it is important to realize you need to throw out your old concept of forgiveness in order to see a new way.

The other aspect of this false forgiveness is asking God to forgive you or another person. God knows what you think you see as an attack never really happened – it's just an illusion. God as Pure Love can never see anything you do as wrong. You are now and always will be perfect in God's eyes. What would God need to forgive you for?

Ask not to be forgiven, for this has already been accomplished. Ask, rather, to learn how to forgive, and to restore what always was to your unforgiving mind (T-14.IV.3).

Once again this attempt to ask God for forgiveness is just another tool of the ego, reinforcing the belief you are guilty. Only by eliminating guilt will you begin to free yourself from the hold of the ego, and the way to eliminate that guilt is by learning the true method of forgiveness.

What Forgiveness Is

As we did in our first discussion about guilt, we will begin our look at true forgiveness by presenting a definition. In this case we will define forgiveness in three ways – one each for past, present, and future:

Forgiveness is realizing the illusion you believed in never happened.

Forgiveness is realizing the illusion you believe in does not exist.

Forgiveness is realizing the illusion you fear will not occur.

Now let's break these definitions apart to better understand what is going on. First we see the word 'realizing' which means that forgiveness is a process of understanding and therefore is purely a process of the mind. Forgiveness does not require any external action whatsoever and believing that such action is required will negate the whole process.

The second word of note is 'illusion' and once again this is in the mind. In a moment we will look more closely at all the different kinds of illusions one might forgive, but for now we will use the simple definition – an illusion is any non-loving thought. It is these non-loving thoughts that we are forgiving, whether they are about the external world we believe we live in or about ourselves.

Next the definition points out that these illusions are simply something you believe in or fear, again purely of the mind. The ego presents a picture of the world and we have believed in that vision and we fear what the future of this world may be. The rules you believe in form the basis for this world and the basis for all the guilt and fear in this world.

Finally the crux of forgiveness is that these illusions never happened, do not exist, and will not occur. Once you accept that, the forgiveness is complete, and once the forgiveness is complete the illusion will be gone, leaving peace in its place.

Only illusions can be forgiven, and then they disappear. Forgiveness is release from all illusions... (T-24.III.1).

With our definition in mind, let's explore further some of these non-loving thoughts. These are all the thoughts, feelings, and emotions the ego presents to us so we will keep focused on the projected external illusory world. Any thought or feeling about anyone or any event that is not truly unconditional love will be considered a non-loving thought.

For example, any thoughts that include guilt, attack, pain, sickness, fear, worry, anxiety, death, or even mild discomfort or unease, are non-loving thoughts. Obviously this includes a broad range, and in fact, what it really includes is almost every thought you have in your daily life. This means there is a lot of mental material available to you in order to practice forgiveness. As we go through the rest of this chapter, we'll see how to address these thoughts one by one.

For now, what is important to remember is that this way of forgiveness as presented to us by the Course is entirely a process of changing your mind.

> Therefore, seek not to change the world, but choose to change your mind about the world (T-21.Intro.1).

By choosing to change your mind about the ego's illusions, wherever you see them, you will begin to free yourself from the ego and all of its non-loving thoughts. What you will discover is that as you forgive these thoughts, the loving thoughts that are who you really are, will come naturally to the surface and will eventually push away the ego's thoughts. A true transformation will begin.

The Holy Spirit

We first looked at the concept of the Holy Spirit in Chapter 4. There we learned that the Holy Spirit is the part of the separated self that remembers the Mind of God. As we stated, there is nothing unique about the name Holy Spirit, and if you prefer to call it something else, that is fine. Names are not important to the Course.

What is important is that this part of us, this place within our minds, is the connection between the separated world we believe in and the Home within the Mind of God our True Self has never left. Since we believe so thoroughly in all the illusions the ego has presented to us, we need help in finding our way to forgiveness. The Holy Spirit offers that help. The Course refers to the Holy Spirit as our Communication Link between the illusory world of the ego and the real world of God.

> Being the Communication Link between God and [the separated self], the Holy Spirit interprets everything you have made in the light of what He is. The ego separates

through the body. The Holy Spirit reaches through it to others (T-8.VII.2).

The Communication Link that God Himself placed within you, joining your mind with His, cannot be broken (T-13.XI.8).

The Holy Spirit offers us a bridge back to our True Home, and it is through this bridge that we will be able to release all of our illusions. The Holy Spirit, being true to God, is never judgmental about these illusions. Whatever illusion you bring, whether seemingly minor or horrendous, will instantly disappear.

Because the ego will always try to prevent us from realizing true forgiveness, we need to be able to access the Holy Spirit within our minds in order to forgive. The best way to do this is to find a way to quiet your mind, to turn off the constant ego thoughts that keep this world spinning. Try to take a few minutes every day when you can be away from the noise and clamor of normal life, and find the still place within.

Simply sit in this place and relax and breathe easily and say to yourself, "I want to touch the Holy Spirit within my mind." Repeat it slowly and as you do look around within your mind for a place that feels more peaceful. When you find that place, turn your attention there and continue to repeat the phrase. As you do this over time, you will find you will be naturally drawn to the place of peace within, and you will know you are reaching the bridge to your True Home, the Holy Spirit.

The Holy Spirit, like the ego, is a decision. Together they constitute all the alternatives the mind can accept and obey. The Holy Spirit and the ego are the only choices open to you. God created one, and so you cannot eradicate it. You made the other, and so you can. Only what God creates is irreversible and unchangeable (T-5.V.6).

So in order to truly forgive, you must connect with the Holy Spirit, since it is through this channel that we can see the ego's illusions for what they are. We will see that the first step in forgiveness is to take a moment and touch the place in your mind where the Holy Spirit resides. Once you've made the contact, then you can proceed with the process of forgiveness.

> Forgiveness through the Holy Spirit lies simply in looking beyond error from the beginning, and thus keeping it unreal for you... What has no effect does not exist, and to the Holy Spirit the effects of error are nonexistent. By steadily and consistently canceling out all its effects, everywhere and in all respects, He teaches that the ego does not exist and proves it (T-9.IV.5).

Now we are ready to learn the process of forgiveness, which can lead us to a regular practice. This practice will, over time, eat away at the barriers the ego has assembled to keep you from experiencing the fundamental Love that is yours. We will move closer with each instance of forgiveness to our True Home.

> Follow the Holy Spirit's teaching in forgiveness, then, because forgiveness is His function and He knows how to fulfill it perfectly (T-9.IV.6).

The Practice of Forgiveness

Before we can practice forgiveness, we must first learn how to forgive, a technique we can repeat over and over to hone our skills of forgiveness. In reading the Course, the process of forgiveness is presented in various ways, but for our purposes we'll focus on a specific technique that can be used repeatedly in many different situations.

This will involve three basic steps. As we just discussed, the first is to learn to connect with the Holy Spirit within our minds. Next we will identify a specific non-loving thought where we know forgiveness is required. Finally we will apply a simple procedure to forgive, using the help of the Holy Spirit to overcome any resistance.

Step 1 – Connecting with the Holy Spirit

We begin our process by learning how to connect with the Holy Spirit. The Holy Spirit is simply the part of our selves that remembers our connection to God, the part of us that knows only Truth and knows only Love.

The first task on the path to forgiveness is to experience the Holy Spirit, a little glimpse of the wonder of God. Take a moment and think on that place in your mind where you know there is peace and love available to you. You may initially only be able to feel this place for a fleeting moment, before the ego fills your mind with all of its non-loving thoughts, but by practicing this regularly you will begin more and more to know and feel comfortable in this place.

Step 2 – Identifying a Non-Loving Thought

Once you've made the connection to the Holy Spirit, no matter how small it may seem, you can begin the process of forgiveness. The next step is to identify within your mind a non-loving thought. This can be a thought of anger, fear, guilt, pain, or any other thought where you feel upset or discomfort with someone or yourself or some experience.

So let's try an example. Think about a non-loving thought you've had in the last day or two – any thought with feelings of fear, anger, guilt, etc. associated with it. Bring that thought to the front of your mind, focus on it intently. Feel all the emotions surrounding it. If possible, imagine those emotions as something physical, like a dark, roiling ball of ugliness.

Step 3 – Forgiving the Experience

Now holding that focus, begin to forgive everything associated with this experience. We have learned from the Course that all these feelings and thoughts are illusions presented to us by our egos. Knowing this, forgive each person with any connection to these thoughts, saying "I forgive..." followed by the person's name, repeating it several times. Then forgive the experience itself, saying "I forgive..." followed by what you call the event, and then "... knowing this is just an illusion created by my ego."

Next take that roiling ball of ugliness, with all the emotions tied into this experience and hand it off to the Holy Spirit, who remembers the Mind of God and knows these emotions and thoughts are illusions with no power whatsoever. This releases the experience, the emotions, and the non-loving false thoughts. The ego loses some of its hold on you as your awareness of the Holy Spirit reminds you of where you belong.

As one final step, say "I forgive myself", for it was you, as your ego self, that had all these thoughts and emotions originally. By forgiving yourself you release yourself from the heavy weight of responsibility for this negative experience, and because of this, you will naturally feel closer to the Holy Spirit.

When you have completed this, try selecting another non-loving thought and follow the same procedure. In this case you might try something further in the past, perhaps something in a relationship that has bothered you for years. The process is the same no matter when the thought and associated emotions first occurred. It's still an illusion and the Holy Spirit stands ready to release you from it.

Now you're ready to begin a regular practice. Set aside a brief time every day to forgive a few of your non-loving thoughts. After awhile, you can increase this process to several times a day as it becomes more and more natural. Eventually you may find yourself doing it without having to think about it too seriously.

Once this daily practice becomes second nature, you can begin to apply the technique in real-time to events in your life. The ultimate goal is for you to realize when non-loving thoughts occur and to instantly forgive them. This can lead to a state of continual forgiveness, a state where every unpleasant experience in your life is immediately turned around through forgiveness.

Think about it. All the fear, pain, anger, sadness, and guilt that you've felt over the years being instantly forgiven. This state of continual forgiveness will lead to the state of Peace the Course talks about, for if all your non-loving thoughts are being forgiven, the ego has lost its hold on you, and all that will be left is Love.

You will experience resistance along the way, for the ego will not let go easily. So it's important that you maintain your intent and focus in order to overcome the obstacles placed in your way. You must put forgiveness into practice, applying it to all the events of your life, if you want to free yourself from the ego's hold.

Examples of Guilt and Forgiveness

Now once again we visit our four examples of guilt. It is time to take the feelings of guilt from these examples and show how we can apply the process of forgiveness to each one. We will look at the "ego ideals", the rules that each of these individuals believes in, and see how these are just illusions. Through this realization these individuals can become free of the guilt impacting their lives.

We are assuming that each of these individuals shows some willingness to forgive, some intention to see the world in a different way.

Offer the Holy Spirit only your willingness to remember, for He retains the knowledge of God and of yourself for you, waiting for your acceptance (T-10.II.2).

The Holy Spirit's Voice is as loud as your willingness to listen (T-8.VIII.8).

Without this willingness, true forgiveness cannot occur, for that would be a choice in favor of the ego. The willingness need not be complete, but we must take the first step and then the Holy Spirit can take us the rest of the way.

As we go through these examples and see these people losing their guilt, you may feel as if they are getting away with something. Clearly it appears they have done something wrong and we might blame them for their actions and want them to feel guilty. In the next chapter, we will address this feeling that by eliminating guilt, we are getting away with whatever we did. For now, just know that if each of these individuals makes a true effort to forgive with the help of the Holy Spirit, the guilt will fade away and this is ok.

Example 1: Sarah is feeling guilty because she lost control of her anger and lashed out at her sister, and also because she feels she has failed to achieve success in life. She felt she was violating two internal rules – the first that she should never show anger toward another person and the second concerning her belief in being a failure at life.

There are actually three illusions Sarah needs to forgive here. The first is that her sister is guilty of being angry with her or not loving her enough. The second is Sarah's anger toward her sister, and the last is her guilt over not achieving in life. It is important to note that in the ego's world, anger is an attempt to make someone else feel guilty. In the Holy Spirit's world, anger is just another non-loving thought, just another illusion to be forgiven.

So we will assume that Sarah is now a student of the Course and wants to look at her life from a new perspective. She has been taking time each day to touch the Holy Spirit in her mind. She has begun to forgive some of the little things in her life. Now she sits down, connects to the Holy Spirit, and calls up all her feelings about her sister – the anger her sister shows her, the anger she returns to her sister, and her feelings that her sister is right about her failures.

This is painful for her, bringing up anger, guilt, sadness, longing, loss, a whole host of non-loving thoughts. Feeling these emotions to their fullest, she calls on the Holy Spirit to sweep them away, as she says "I forgive my sister for everything, knowing what she has done is just an ego illusion." Then "I forgive myself for believing all these negative things about my sister and myself, for these also are illusions."

She stays in this place, repeating the phrases over and over, keeping in touch with the Holy Spirit, sending these waves of emotion off to disappear. If this is done with sincerity and focus, she will feel a new lightness, a peacefulness toward her sister and within herself. She is breaking through an important ego barrier, and releasing some of her guilt.

Example 2: Michael is feeling guilty about the affair he is having with a colleague at work. He is also feeling guilty about having to lie to his wife. He is violating his own internal rules about fidelity in marriage and about honesty with someone he loves.

Michael needs to forgive the special relationship he has with his wife, so the true unconditional love can shine through. He needs to forgive himself for looking outside his marriage for answers, for having an affair, and for lying to his wife about it. The future of his marriage may still be unknown, but as long as the relationship continues to be built on unrealistic expectations, lies, and guilt, it cannot be a healthy relationship.

So Michael has discovered the Course and this unique method of forgiveness. He takes some time to find and experience the Holy Spirit within himself. He wants to forgive these relationships and his feelings of guilt. While connecting to the Holy Spirit, he focuses on his wife and the conditions they have both put on the marriage. He feels all the discomfort, pain, guilt, and anger that has grown in their years together.

Now feeling these emotions intensely, he says, "I forgive my wife for all the pain I believe she caused, for it was only an illusion." "I forgive myself for inflicting pain in the relationship, for this was an illusion as well." He then passes off to the Holy Spirit these non-loving feelings, as he repeats the phrases over and over. He begins to feel a new lightness and a new comfort with his wife.

Finally he focuses on the deceit, lying, and dishonesty surrounding his affair, and he says, "I forgive myself for my deceit and lying and for the resulting guilt I've felt." All the non-loving thoughts are passed to the Holy Spirit again and he feels some of the guilt lifting away. He doesn't know where his two relationships are headed, but he is beginning to understand that ultimately this is not up to any ego decision of his. If he is willing to listen to the Holy Spirit regularly, his path will become clear.

Example 3: David is feeling guilty about not having done enough for his dying mother. He has a great many responsibilities in his life – work, wife, children – and he doesn't believe he has the time and financial resources to satisfy everyone.

David learns about the Course, but feels he cannot devote enough time to it with all his commitments. His ego doesn't want him to turn his attention away from the projected world that's been presented to him, but eventually he realizes something must change with all the stress and guilt in his life. He somehow finds a few moments of free time to discover the Holy Spirit within.

Once he does, he thinks about the guilt that has been heaped on him since childhood. He looks at the guilt he has tried to induce in his children and others in order to try to get away from some of his own guilt. He focuses intently, feeling the guilt and the pain, his own as well as that of others. He says, "I forgive all the people in my life who have tried to induce guilt in me, for that was only an illusion." "I forgive myself for feeling the guilt from these people." "Finally I forgive myself for trying to make others feel guilty, for there is no reason for this guilt."

The Holy Spirit is called upon to take away all these layers of guilt, as he repeats his forgiveness statements. Suddenly he begins to see the people in his life in a new light, a light of love instead of the darkness of guilt. He realizes he can break the chain of generational guilt if he will just stay on this new course of forgiveness.

Example 4: Melissa decides to drive her friend, Susan, home from a party, knowing she has had too much to drink. The tragic conclusion results in a wave of guilt – from Susan's family, from the community, from the legal system, and Melissa's own internal guilt.

In Melissa's case we find layer upon layer of complex guilt, coming at her from many different directions, along with the internal guilt she feels. In this case we have to take forgiveness to a new level. We have to show how someone's death, seemingly caused by another, is really an illusion. The ego will fight with every ounce of its strength against this, because the fear of death is one of its most powerful illusions.

So let's assume now that Melissa has been found legally guilty for the act, and that Susan's family, and the wider community at large feel she is guilty. Melissa feels this guilt coming toward her as she also feels her own sense of responsibility for what happened. It feels like a tremendous weight, pushing her down, deeper inside herself. Depression now develops alongside the guilt, and she begins to cut herself off from others.

But somewhere along the way someone who cares about her tells her about the Course and she begins to look at the possibility of lifting some of this guilt. Ripped away from her normal life, she has time to contemplate, but initially the pain of it is too great. She does begin, though, to spend a little time each day trying to connect to the Holy Spirit, just looking for a place of comfort within.

As she makes this connection, she starts to look at this mountain of guilt, trying her best to feel the weight of it. She knows this is a necessary step before she can be free of it. Then one day, as she connects with her inner guide, she says "I forgive all those in the world who have judged me guilty, for I know this guilt is an illusion." "I forgive myself for feeling all that guilt, knowing it is preventing me from seeing the love in the world."

She passes those feelings of guilt and depression and pain to the Holy Spirit, believing for the first time it can all disappear. Then she approaches the big one. "I forgive myself and everyone else for believing in Susan's death, for I know her mind is eternal." The ego has created the illusion of Susan's body and Melissa's body and our bodies as well. The death of the body is just an illusion of an illusion. As she passes the pain she feels about Susan's death to the Holy Spirit, she becomes infused with the love she had for Susan. She may still miss Susan's presence in this world, but she is beginning to realize Susan never really left.

Forgiving Your Guilt and the Guilt of Others

In this final section of the chapter, we'll now focus on you. This is where you will take the process of forgiveness we have learned and apply it to specific examples of guilt in your life. This will be the way you will, in a very personal way, take those instances of guilt you feel, both within yourself and toward others, and with the help of the Holy Spirit, forgive them one by one.

> There is another advantage – and a very important one – in referring decisions to the Holy Spirit with increasing frequency... To follow the Holy Spirit's guidance is to let yourself be absolved of guilt... It is the core of the curriculum... To return the function to the One to Whom it belongs is thus the escape from fear. And it is this that lets the memory of love return to you (M-29.3).

So let's begin the process of absolving your guilt. One of the best ways to start this is to write a list of all the things in your life you feel guilty about. Then write another list of all the things and people in the world that you believe are guilty. These lists should range widely, catching guilt with those very close to you and with those far removed, like criminals and people in power.

The lists should also cover a wide range of time. Start with events that have happened recently, maybe starting with today and working backward one day at a time. Then occasionally leap to the events from your past that hold the most powerful guilty feelings for you. Then think about possible future events you are worried may have guilt associated with them.

Let the list grow naturally, revisiting it regularly, not worrying about how long it is or whether you might be missing something important. It does not matter at all how many items are on the list or if the items seem trivial or profound. Each instance of forgiveness is the same, for with each instance you have made a decision to move closer to God.

Now with these lists in hand, take some time each day, just ten minutes or so if that's all you can spare, and begin the practice of forgiveness. You can pick something completely at random or something that is particularly troubling to you. Take a few moments to go to a quiet, relaxed place and try to experience the presence of the Holy Spirit in your mind.

To whatever degree you feel that presence, focus on it and follow the process of forgiveness we discussed above. Take an item from the list and say "I forgive the guilt I feel about..." the item, or if appropriate, "I forgive the person who I believe is guilty." Take all the feelings of guilt and pain and sadness associated with the event or person, and hand it to the waiting Holy Spirit, to disappear as the illusion it is.

Finally say "I forgive myself for having these feelings of guilt." With the Holy Spirit, there is no blame, no judgment, only acceptance. Pass to the Holy Spirit any lingering feelings of guilt, and realize the true release of forgiveness. Once this is done, don't delete the item, just make a mark or note by the item on the list. This will show your progress on the path to forgiveness.

After you have done this for awhile, you will have many marks by the items on your list. Now when you reread those marked items, you should have an entirely different emotional reaction toward them. If you have truly forgiven in the way we just discussed, the attachment you had to those items will have melted away. It is through this accumulation of marked items that your emotional freedom will grow.

As you continue to add new items to the list, and you practice forgiveness and mark items off, you may find that items that you haven't yet forgiven and that were strongly emotional for you, may no longer hold such attachment. Once you start forgiveness for some items, that forgiveness will naturally spread to others without making conscious effort. The Holy Spirit can continue to work in the background, and the fact you are giving this process your attention increases the forgiveness in your life.

In the next chapter, we'll look at the consequences of a regular practice of forgiveness moving toward that ideal of continual forgiveness. We will look at what it will be like to be without guilt, to be guiltless, and to see the world around you as guiltless as well. The changes can be profound, but are as natural as your breath, for as you start on the journey of forgiveness, you are simply on a path back to your True Home.

All this beauty will rise to bless your sight as you look upon the world with forgiving eyes. For forgiveness literally transforms vision, and lets you see the real world reaching quietly and gently across chaos, removing all illusions that had twisted your perception and fixed it on the past. The smallest leaf becomes a thing of wonder, and a blade of grass a sign of God's perfection (T-17.II.6).

For further study in the Course on how forgiveness can release us from guilt, refer to Chapter 16, "The Forgiveness of Illusions" and Chapter 17, "Forgiveness and the Holy Relationship".

Chapter 7

The Guiltless Life

Let's review where we have come so far. We began with our simple definition of guilt, looking at different examples of guilt and shame. We explored guilt in a historical context, examining the religious, philosophical, and psychological belief systems in which guilt plays a role. We looked at how we build our internal belief system, all the rules we use to make decisions, the rules that govern our behavior.

Then as an alternative to this rules-based view of the world, we introduced the philosophy of the Course. Within this philosophy we examined the concept of guilt, seeing it as a central part of the ego's illusion. We discovered that these rules we live by are actually presented to us by the ego. Finally we learned how, through forgiveness, we can release the ego's vision of the world, and free ourselves of our guilt and the guilt we see in others.

Once we start on this path of forgiveness, we will be chipping away at the ego's edifice of guilt. We will be making the transition from being guilty to being guiltless. This is a process and can be thought of as an arc taking us from one side to the other over time. Viewed from the guilt side of the arc, it may be difficult to see what it means to be guiltless, so we will now try to give a hint of what that life would be like.

Continual Forgiveness

In the early stages of your practice, instances of true forgiveness may be few and far between, but as long as you maintain the willingness, progress will be made. Over time, this practice will become more natural to you as you begin to observe how even small instances of forgiveness can change your emotional life. As you work through your personal list of guilt, each time one for-giveness occurs, your path to remembrance has been shortened.

As you proceed, at some point along the way an event will occur in your life that will cause non-loving thoughts in your mind. You may suddenly realize, "Why not forgive this right now?" In that moment, walking down the street or in a crowded room, you call on the Holy Spirit inside and follow the process of for-giveness. You have changed your mind about the event, so that instant of guilt or anger you felt will fade away almost immedi-ately.

The next time you recognize one of these non-loving thoughts, you will remember how you were previously able to remove one of these with this instant forgiveness. Now it becomes easier to do it again, and the next time it will be even easier. Each time you forgive, you build on the last forgiveness until it becomes a completely natural process to you.

Now you have taken the first steps on the path to a life of con-tinual forgiveness. What this means is that in addition to taking time to work through your list of past instances of guilt, you have added new acts of forgiveness taking place as you live your everyday life. You will begin to realize that you can live your life at the same time you are freeing yourself from the ego through forgiveness. There no longer needs to be a separation between your usual busy life and your inner life of forgiveness.

You are now on the road to this state of continual forgiveness, where every non-loving thought is looked at in real-time and instantly forgiven. When you get there, the ego will be in its final throes. All the non-loving thoughts it tries to throw at you will no longer stick. They appear, are forgiven, and then disappear. What is left are the loving thoughts that are the basis of who you really are, the loving thoughts that are your birthright as a child of God.

Of course, like so many things in this separated world, this whole process is not a straight line. There will be times you will fall back into ego ways of thinking, only to rise again to remember your practice of forgiveness. Be assured though, as long as you maintain a clear intent, a willingness, the Holy Spirit will make sure you find your way Home. When things seem to take a wrong turn, simply stop for a few moments and call on the Holy Spirit to help you see the way back onto your path.

Being Guiltless

Our goal from the beginning of this book is to outline a process through which we can all reach the end of guilt. We first learned how the source of our guilt is not in the external world, but from the ego within. Once we make that identification, it is then possible, with the help of the Holy Spirit to forgive the guilt we see outside and inside as well. Through constant practice we can reach that place of instant forgiveness, leading to living our lives in a state of continual forgiveness.

Until forgiveness is complete, the world does have a purpose. It becomes the home in which forgiveness is born, and where it grows and becomes stronger and more all-embracing. Here is it nourished, for here it is needed (M-14.2).

In a state of continual forgiveness, guilt ultimately cannot survive. No matter how hard the ego tries to maintain our sense of separation, it will be met immediately by the power of forgiveness. Eventually the ego will shrink and fade, and in its place will be a guiltless life. The world will look different without guilt in it. The world will not instantly disappear, but it will become a place of beauty and love, and you will look on those around you as no longer separate.

A fundamental part of a guiltless life is the elimination of fear.

If I am guiltless, I have nothing to fear (T-14.III.3).

The outcome of the lesson that God's Son is guiltless is a world in which there is no fear, and everything is lit with hope and sparkles with a gentle friendliness (T-31.I.8).

The End of Guilt

When you no longer feel guilty, you will no longer project guilt onto the world, and will therefore no longer perceive guilt in the world. When neither you nor anyone you come in contact with is guilty, there truly is nothing to fear. Imagine a world without fear, a world without death. This is the final result of a world without guilt.

Remember back to the idea of the original guilt the ego presented to us, the guilt we felt for seemingly having separated from God. This was the ego's original tool for trapping us in this idea of separation. When we have finally forgiven this last instance of guilt, the ego will no longer have a leg to stand on. The end of guilt is the end of the ego and the end of the ego is the end of guilt.

With this new guiltless view of the world, you can become a teacher through your example of living a life of continual forgiveness.

There is a course for every teacher of God. The form of the course varies greatly. But the content of the course never changes. Its central theme is always, "God's Son is guiltless, and in his innocence is his salvation." It can be taught by actions or thoughts; in words or soundlessly; in any language or in no language; in any place or time or manner (M-1.3).

This teaching does not require that you change the circumstances of your life, but only that you continue your practice of forgiveness. As you listen to the Holy Spirit, you will find that you will be naturally guided in certain directions that will allow you to fulfill your function as a teacher. The curriculum of your teaching will always be forgiveness.

And finally a world without guilt will be a world without death. If we are transformed into a remembrance of our True Home in the Mind of God, we will remember our True Self is eternal as well. All the pain and attack and death the ego used to send our way is lost when guilt is lost.

Teacher of God, your one assignment could be stated thus: Accept no compromise in which death plays a part... What seems to die has but been misperceived and carried to illusion. Now it becomes your task to let the illusion be carried to the truth... And what is the end of death? Nothing but this; the realization that the Son of God is guiltless now and forever. Nothing but this. But do not let yourself forget it is not less than this (M-27.7).

You can and will become guiltless through the practice of forgiveness. It only requires that little willingness and a simple understanding of what to do. Everything you need to learn is in the Course and in this book. All that is required is for you to take action and begin looking for your non-loving thoughts and with the help of the Holy Spirit, forgiving those thoughts one by one. The state of being guiltless is yours.

A New Moral Code

In the early chapters of this book, we showed how our everyday lives are dominated by the rules we believe in. Wherever those rules came from, the sum total of these make up some kind of moral code we live by. This code may come from hard and fast religious rules, or may be something you have developed through reading and experience. In any case, this code, this set of rules, is what you call on when making decisions in your life.

But now as you start the process of forgiveness, you may be feeling adrift. For your whole life you have depended on a set of rules, an internal structure of beliefs, that are based on the moral, legal, ethical, and religious rules of the world around you. These rules brought some sense of certainty to your life and without them the ground under you may seem less secure.

What can replace these rules, this moral code, this sense of certainty and security in your life? It's simply the practice of forgiveness. We know that as we forgive, we are eradicating non-loving thoughts and letting our natural love come through. As we do this, we will become kinder and more loving toward those around us, realizing they are no longer guilty as we are no longer guilty. The crutch of our internal rules only prevents us from living a truly peaceful, loving life.

Ultimately you will no longer have to live by a set of rules. When you are truly connected to the Holy Spirit, you will be guided in your life to seek and act in the most Loving way possible. The Holy Spirit does not impose rules – the Holy Spirit simply Loves. Each time you forgive, you open your heart wider. As you forgive more and more, you will also begin to simply Love, and eventually you will see those rules you thought you needed to live were a cage imprisoning you.

By working toward the goal of continual forgiveness, you are moving along a path where the ego's influence begins to fade. In its place is a sense of Love and Peace with everyone in this world and with your Loving God. The illusions of the world will fall away. How this will happen is unknown for any particular individual, but the Holy Spirit will guide you where you need to go, and that place will always be the most Loving place possible.

Rethinking Our World

Once we approach this state of guiltlessness with this new moral code of forgiveness, the way we perceive the world around us will change. We may find ourselves rethinking many past beliefs, whether we learned these as we were growing up from our parents, our teachers, or our religious leaders, or simply in observation of the world around us. We will look on these teachings that were so central to us in a new way, finding that we have to reject so many of them, especially ones that have guilt associated with them.

For instance, many believe that if you feel anger you should try to suppress it, and others feel it is important to express your anger. In the Course, anger is always an attempt to make another feel guilty. If you are truly guiltless, you will have no guilt to project onto another, and therefore will never feel angry. If you are feeling angry, it doesn't matter whether you suppress it or express it. What matters is that you recognize it as another non-loving thought, just another opportunity for forgiveness. Eventually anger, like all other non-loving thoughts, will simply fade away.

As another example, there is the concept in psychology that a little bit of guilt is a good thing since it prevents us from acting in destructive ways. What this concept says is that we should always act with a little bit of fear of the consequences. But a little bit of guilt means the ego is still active, doing its job of maintaining the separation. Its telling us we should still refer to those rules, those "ego ideals", in order to make our decisions, allowing it to maintain its power over us.

What the Course says is we should forgive this little remaining guilt and fear and become, once and for all, guiltless. This is the only state that will lead us back Home to our place in the Loving Mind of God. Anything short of guiltlessness means forgiveness is not complete, and incomplete forgiveness means we are not guiltless.

> Perhaps you are accustomed to using guiltlessness merely to offset the pain of guilt, and do not look upon it as having value in itself. You believe that guilt and guiltlessness are both of value, each representing an escape from what the other does not offer you. You do not want either alone, for without both you do not see yourself as whole and therefore happy. Yet you are whole only in your guilt-lessness, and only in your guiltlessness can you be happy. There is no conflict here. To wish for guilt in any way, in any form, will lose appreciation of the value of your guilt-lessness, and push it from your sight (T-14.III.2).

There is a simple logic at work here. If you are in a place of forgiveness and without guilt, you cannot project attack onto the world. If you are projecting attack onto the world, you are not without guilt. Attack and guiltlessness cannot exist together, nor can fear and guiltlessness, nor indeed guilt and guiltlessness. If you want guiltlessness, all these non-loving thoughts must be gone, and through forgiveness they can be gone.

Much of the ego's strange behavior is directly attributable to its definition of guilt. To the ego, *the guiltless are guilty*. Those who do not attack are its "enemies" because, by not valuing its interpretation of salvation, they are in an excellent position to let it go. They have approached the darkest and deepest cornerstone in the ego's foundation, and while the ego can withstand your raising all else to question, it guards this one secret with its life, for its existence depends on keeping this secret. So it is this secret that we must look upon, for the ego cannot protect you against truth, and in its presence the ego is dispelled (T-13.II.4).

You now have the tools to dispel the ego, to remove guilt and fear and pain from your life, to begin to experience the Peace and Love the Holy Spirit wishes for you. You can begin your practice of forgiveness any time, but the longer you wait, the longer you will experience the ego's world. Ultimately time is irrelevant, since our True Home is eternal, but as long as you have some guilt left in you, as long as you see your body living in an external world, it will take time to forgive.

But know this with absolute certainty. Once you start on the path of forgiveness, once you show that little willingness to the Holy Spirit, once you begin to dispel your non-loving thoughts, nothing outside your mind can stop you. Your willingness is your salvation, your willingness is your path to the end of the ego, your willingness will lead you to being guiltless, and your willingness will lead us all to the end of guilt.

For further study in the Course on what a guiltless world would be like, refer to Chapter 13, "The Guiltless World" and Chapter 14, Section III, "The Decision for Guiltlessness".

Chapter 8

The End of Guilt

We began this journey back in the ego's world, a world dominated by rules and consequences for violating those rules, a world permeated with guilt and fear and pain, a world of separation, one from the other. We looked on that world and found it wanting. We chose to think differently about the world, to see it as an illusion maintained by this thing we call the ego. We looked inside and discovered the Holy Spirit waiting for our return, waiting to help us forgive.

We learned how to see this illusion for what it is, to forgive the non-loving thoughts the ego throws our way. As this process continued, one forgiveness after another, we began to see those we share this world with as guiltless, just as we are guiltless. Once we saw that light of guiltlessness on the horizon, we were inexorably drawn to it, accelerating our process of forgiveness.

Now we are guiltless, now we are at peace, now we share our peacefulness with the world, expressing love to all we come in contact with. As we are joined by others, as forgiveness permeates the world, we approach the end of guilt. No longer will guilt be used to keep us from our Home, from the remembrance of the Mind of God. That long carpet of the past will roll up behind us, and there will only be the perfect present.

This is what the end of guilt means. This is why we are on the journey of forgiveness. This is what that small willingness you started with will grow into. Love is our birthright, from our birth as a Child of God. Love is inevitable and has only been so briefly hidden from us as we took this momentary wrong turn along the way. Now we have found the signposts pointing us in the right direction, the signposts of forgiveness and guiltlessness.

The End of Guilt

The world we are returning to is unrecognizable to those who have lived with guilt, but this is the world that is waiting for you. You can make those first simple steps that will lead you on a path to freedom – freedom from guilt, freedom from fear, freedom from the ego that has dominated your life.

Say good-by now to the ego and all his tricks and illusions. Say farewell to this world we have struggled through for so long. Say so long to all the non-loving thoughts that have filled your mind.

Say hello to the brightness of this new world. Say welcome to all who join you on this journey. And say thank you to the Loving God who never sees guilt, only perfection, the perfection of the life we now return to.

> This world of light, this circle of brightness is the real world, where guilt meets with forgiveness. Here the world outside is seen anew, without the shadow of guilt upon it. Here are you forgiven, for here you have forgiven everyone. Here is the new perception, where everything is bright and shining with innocence, washed in the waters of forgiveness, and cleansed of every evil thought you laid upon it. Here there is no attack upon the Son of God, and you are welcome. Here is your innocence, waiting to clothe you and protect you, and make you ready for the final step in the journey inward. Here are the dark and heavy garments of guilt laid by, and gently replaced by purity and love (T-18.IX.9).

Suggested Reading

For further study of *A Course in Miracles*,

> *A Course in Miracles*, Second Edition, Foundation for Inner Peace, www.acim.org

> Navarro, Edwin, *It's All Mind: The Simplified Philosophy of A Course in Miracles*, Navarro Publishing, www.edwinnavarro.com

> Wapnick, Kenneth, *The Message of A Course in Miracles*, *Vol. 1, All Are Called*, Foundation for *A Course in Miracles*, www.facim.org

Contact the author at www.edwinnavarro.com.

Made in the USA
Monee, IL
02 December 2024

71782645R00066